FREEDOM *from* CATHOLICISM

A Guidebook for Those Who are Searching

MARY ANN COLLINS

WAGNER
PUBLICATIONS

Freedom from Catholicism
Copyright ©2002 by Wagner Publications
ISBN 1-58502-033-8
Library of Congress Control Number: 2002113334

Portions written by Mary Ann Collins (including the Glossary, Appendix 1, and Appendix 2), Copyright ©2002 by Mary Ann Collins. Used by permission.
www.freedomfromcatholicism.com

Published by
Wagner Publications
11005 N. Highway 83
Colorado Springs, CO 80921
www.wagnerpublications.org

Cover design by
Keith Sherrer
iDesignEtc.
Email: idesignetc@qwest.net

Rights for publishing this book in other languages are contracted by Gospel Literature International (GLINT). GLINT also provides technical help for the adaptation, translation, and publishing of Bible study resources and books in scores of languages worldwide. For further information, contact GLINT, P.O. Box 4060, Ontario, CA 91761-1003, USA. You may also send e-mail to glintint@aol.com, or visit their web site at www.glint.org.

1   2   3   4   5   6   7   8   9   08   07   06   05   04   03   02

TABLE
of
CONTENTS

INTRODUCTION

by

C. PETER WAGNER

We live in a rapidly-changing world. Religion, while characterized by sociologists as one of the more conservative of human institutions, is no longer exempt from the changes that are occurring. For many, the status quo has little appeal. Due to today's unprecedented diffusion of information through the electronic superhighway, an increasing number of religious people are beginning to ask new questions concerning the religion of their parents. Previous generations, for the most part, assumed that their religion, similar to their DNA, was simply a given of life. But no longer.

CHANGES AMONG CATHOLICS

Roman Catholicism, the most traditional of Christian groupings, has painfully experienced the results of this new freedom, especially in the past two or three decades. In the U.S., for example, the dramatically increasing shortage of ordained clergy in the Catholic Church has been making national news. The exposure of rampant sexual abuse among many of those who remain in the priesthood has aggravated the problem. A growing number of Catholics are now wondering if there may not be better options which could allow them to serve God on a higher level.

One of the characteristics of Roman Catholicism, and this, of course, also applies to most religious systems, is a desire to keep the faithful in the fold. A common way of accomplishing this objective is to create a religious environment in which members develop a strong fear of questioning the status quo. Partly because of its unmatched historical longevity, the Roman Catholic Church through the years has developed finely-tuned skills designed to retain its members. For the most part they have been successful. The result is that most Catholics are literally captives of a religious system that they have inherited from their parents. Today, however, a growing number of them have a heartfelt desire to escape that religious captivity and to enter into a true freedom in Christ.

LATIN AMERICA

Nowhere has this been more evident than in Latin America. My wife, Doris, and I had the privilege of serving as field missionaries to Bolivia for sixteen years. We experienced the pre-Vatican II wrath of Catholic leaders in public confrontations, stonings, and even spending time in jail. We knew full well that the great majority of those who depended on the Church, on Mary, or on the saints for their salvation had never been born again and therefore, according to Jesus, could never see the Kingdom of God (see John

3:3). Back in those days, relatively few Catholics were leaving their traditional church.

Now, however, the change has occurred. The Pope himself has expressed alarm at the phenomenon of huge numbers of Catholics becoming evangelicals. It is said that in Brazil, for example, more evangelicals are now in church on a given Sunday than Catholics. Guatemala may well be the first of the Latin American republics to have a majority of its population evangelical. Almost all Latin American evangelicals are ex-Catholics or children of ex-Catholics. I say this because the uniform testimony of these millions of Latin American evangelicals is that while in the Roman Catholic Church they had given allegiance to a religious system that did not lead them to salvation. Looking back, they now know that if they had died while they were still Catholics they would have ended up in hell. They are now in evangelical churches, they have a personal relationship with Jesus Christ, and they are deeply grateful for their freedom from Catholicism.

FREEDOM FROM CATHOLICISM

The purpose of this book, *Freedom from Catholicism*, is to facilitate this trend, not only in Latin America, but also in other parts of the world. One of the individuals who knows first hand what it means to be free from Catholicism is Mary Ann Collins, the author of this book. I have known Mary Ann for years and I have admired her courage, her sharp mind, her obedience to God, and her passion to see multitudes of others find freedom in Christ.

This book is not a theological treatise or a historical monograph. It is a personal word from Mary Ann Collins to others who find themselves still in the Catholic Church but seeking freedom. Throughout, she addresses her words to "you," focusing on individuals who have come to the place where they not only desire a personal relationship with Christ, but also a complete break with any religious spirits or psychological bondages that may have carried over. That is why this book can be seen as one extended prayer with many parts. Each part is a prayer for release from a specific spiritual distortion which has become characteristic of Catholicism. Then Chuck Pierce's afterword will guide readers into sealing their personal application and taking the practical steps necessary to maintain their new allegiance.

A WIDE GATE

It will soon become evident to the reader that this book is not irenic. It is not one more attempt at "ecumenical dialogue." It is rather based on the assumption that the Roman Catholic Church has forfeited any claim to be just another legitimate Christian denomination with a slightly different philosophy of ministry. In my opinion the Catholic Church, as a religious structure, actually prevents people from knowing God personally. It is one of the wide gates that lead to destruction (see Mt. 7:13).

As I say that, I do not pretend to be an expert on Catholicism. I am, however, better informed than most. My years of personal involvement in Latin America have provided a firsthand exposure to a culture molded largely by the Church. As a part of my graduate studies in religion, I concentrated on understanding Catholicism and my Princeton Theological Seminary ThM thesis is on *The Marian Theology of Thomas Aquinas*. I believe that I have accumulated sufficient information through research and dialogue to arrive at the conclusion I expressed just above. And I must reiterate that this is, for me, a final conclusion. By this I mean that I am not particularly interested in further dialogue. I am much more interested in helping people find true salvation.

PAPAL IDOLATRY

One of the last serious dialogues in which I did engage was with a prominent theologian representing the renewal movement in the Roman Catholic Church. I do not feel that it is appropriate to mention his name here. This person was upset by something I wrote implying that the Pope himself was committing the sin of idolatry every time he worshiped an idol representing a counterfeit Mary. I actually see this "Mary" as a deceptive adaptation of a pernicious demonic spirit identified in the Bible as the "Queen of Heaven" (see Jeremiah 7:16-18).

My friend argued that the Pope was not "worshiping" Mary, but that he was only "venerating" Mary. I, of course, did not agree. I wrote, "When an individual bows down to a graven image of a dead person, communicates with that person (presumably with a spirit of the dead), expects that person to answer prayers and petitions, pledges love and allegiance to that person, kisses the statue representing that person, and burns candles and incense to honor that person, this seems to me to be just as authentic worship as we see among the priests of Baal in the Old Testament or the followers of Maximón in Guatemala today."

FOLK CATHOLICISM

The argument moves from there to an attempt to make a distinction between the official teaching of the Church as over against how the Catholic religion actually takes shape among the common people such as we might find, for example, in Latin America.

In response to that, I want to refer to a revealing new book by a Penn State historian of religion, Philip Jenkins. The book is called *The Next Christendom* (Oxford University Press). Here is what Jenkins says:

"Contemporary Hispanic theology raises challenging questions about the whole area of popular religious practices, the world of devotions, processions, and pilgrimages often dismissed by a term like 'folk Catholicism.' In the context of Latin American history, though, these practices are quite central to popular religious identity, and it is no longer acceptable to regard them as simply a dilution of the superior European reality. 'Popular religious expressions of the people' thus become 'the living creed and primary sources of theology.'[1] By European standards, these practices may be flawed or suspect, but whoever said that European criteria were absolutely valid for all times and places? Europe created its own religious identity through a lengthy process of mingling and adaptation."[2]

THE COUNTERFEIT MARY

More ominously, from the point of view of potentially apostate Christianity, is the rapid escalation of devotion to the counterfeit Mary, a.k.a. Queen of Heaven. In fact, Philip Jenkins titles his section on this phenomenon, "The Queen of the South Will Rise Up."[3] She is now being regarded by many prominent Catholic leaders and theologians as a "Co-Redemptrix" or "co-redeemer" alongside of Christ. The August 25, 1997 issue of *Newsweek* reported that in the last four years the Pope had received no fewer than 4,340,429 petitions to proclaim officially that Mary should be regarded by the faithful as a co-redeemer with Christ. Attached to this is a movement to declare her also as "Co-Mediatrix" or a co-mediator. In other words, Mary supposedly mediates between humans and God the same as Christ does. Take your choice!

Some have responded that the Pope has rejected this notion. Nevertheless, the Pope has himself modeled a passionate devotion to Mary. Philip Jenkins observes that in more liberal Northern countries (which would include U.S.A.), Mary has played a smaller role in Catholic devotion. However, "This tendency has been reversed somewhat under the conservative papacy of John Paul II, and at the start of the new millennium remarkable attention is being paid to Marian shrines and visions."[4]

How is the Pope communicating this message to the faithful, especially in Latin America? In 1998 he visited Cuba and proclaimed that *La Virgen de Caridad* is the Queen of Cuba. In 2002 he visited Mexico and canonized Juan Diego, the peasant (whether real or fictitious is still a key question for researchers), who reportedly first saw the vision of the Virgin of Guadalupe. Philip Jenkins says, "There is now talk that the Virgin might be proclaimed as a mediator and co-Savior figure, comparable to Jesus himself, even a fourth member of the Trinity. Such ambitious schemes remain controversial, but demographic trends within the Church make it highly likely that they will be implemented in the coming decades."[5]

BORN-AGAIN CATHOLICS

Few would doubt that there are probably hundreds of thousands of Roman Catholics who are born-again Christians. They have found a personal relationship with Christ not because of the Church, but in spite of the Church. However, as long as they remain in that religious system it will be very difficult for them to fulfill the destiny that God has for them. There are probably hundreds of thousands of other Catholics who may not be born again but who nevertheless are sincere seekers after freedom in Christ. This book is mainly addressed to those two groups of people. If they pray the prayers that Mary Ann Collins suggests, I promise that they will enter into a life of blessing that they have not known before.

Notes

[1] This is a quote from Latin American Catholic theologian, Virgilio P. Elizondo, *Galilean Journey* (Maryknoll NY: Orbis Books, 2000), p. 91.

[2] Philip Jenkins, *The Next Christendom: The Coming of Global Christianity* (London, England: Oxford University Press, 2002), p. 117.

[3] Ibid.

[4] Ibid., p. 118.

[5] Ibid.

BIOGRAPHY
of
MARY ANN COLLINS

(A FORMER CATHOLIC NUN)

I was raised a secular humanist. I was looking for something, but I didn't know what it was. Through the influence of a friend, I started investigating Catholicism during my first year of college. For over a year I met with a priest every week and I studied the books he recommended.

After I became a Catholic, I kept studying the lives of the saints and the teachings of various prominent Catholics. I changed to a Catholic college and majored in religious studies. I often went to Mass several times a week, and sometimes every day.

I entered the convent for several reasons. I wanted to be closer to God and to serve Him more wholeheartedly. I wanted to learn more about God and to spend my life being more intensely focused on Him. And I believed that God wanted me to be a nun.

The convent turned out to be an unhealthy place, both spiritually and emotionally. Our self-imposed penances and other attempts to make ourselves more holy encouraged us to become self-righteous. We were not allowed to have friendships or to be close to any human being. We were taught to be emotionally detached and to love people in a detached, impersonal way.

But that teaching is not biblical. When God said "It is not good that the man should be alone" (Genesis 2:18), He was referring to more than just marriage. The Bible encourages close relationships. No person has ever been closer to God the Father than Jesus was. But He was not emotionally detached. He wept publicly. He was "moved with compassion." He made many statements which showed strong emotions. He had close personal relationships with people. He said that His disciples were His friends — not just servants or followers, but friends. He loved all of the disciples, but three of them (Peter, James, and John) were especially close friends. They were the only ones invited to the Mount of Transfiguration, and the raising of Jairus' daughter from the dead. Jesus and John were such close friends that John was known as the "beloved disciple."

I left the convent after two years, before making vows. I was still a novice, undergoing extensive training and "spiritual formation" in preparation for taking vows. I wore a habit. I was given a new name. I was called "Sister."

Some Catholic apologists have said that because I did not make vows I was not truly a nun. However, the *Catholic Encyclopedia* says that if a novice has joined a religious order (which I did) and has been given a religious habit (which I wore) then they are a monk or nun in the broad sense of the term. Therefore, I refer to myself as a "former nun."

After I left the convent, I was frustrated with the local Catholic churches because I did not see strong faith or zeal for God. In addition, some of the priests preached things which were so contrary to Scripture that they were truly distressing to me. One time when this occurred, I left in the middle of Mass and stood outside in the street, weeping. I pulled myself together and went back in time to take communion.

My parents had become Christians and they were members of a Protestant church. I visited their church and found the solid, scripturally-based teaching I had been hungering for. For years I went to early morning Mass and then went to my parents' church.

Eventually I left the Catholic church and joined my parents' church. In doing so, I finally found the personal relationship with God that I had been looking for all of my life.

FREEDOM *from*
CATHOLICISM

"Beware lest any man spoil [ruin] you through
philosophy and vain deceit, after the tradition of men,
after the rudiments of the world, and not after Christ."
(Colossians 2:8)

B ecoming free from Roman Catholicism involves more than
an intellectual recognition that many of its doctrines are contrary to the Bible. There are also issues of loyalty, fear, and the
habit of obeying the priests and the Pope. These issues sometimes trouble ex-Catholics long after they have left the Catholic
Church.

The Bible says, "Let us **lay aside every weight**, and the sin
which doth so easily beset us, and let us run with patience the
race that is set before us" (Hebrews 12:1, emphasis added).
Weights from Catholicism can be hidden and heavy. The following information and prayers should help you rid yourself of them
so your race is easier to run.

The Catholic Church has a heavy hold on its members. Its teachings and practices continually reinforce the belief that the Catholic Church is indispensable for having a right relationship with God. It seeks to equate faith in the Catholic Church with faith in God, so that to leave Catholicism is made to seem like rejecting God. Many popes (including some in the 20th century), have declared that there is no salvation apart from the Pope and from the Catholic Church. In addition, the Catholic Church declares that people cannot understand the Bible apart from Catholic teaching and tradition.

Even when your mind tells you that Catholic teaching and practice is wrong, something in your inner being tends to hold on. That is why I have included prayers in addition to giving you information. The information will help your understanding. The prayers will help your spirit and emotions find freedom from the grip of Catholicism.

Freedom from Catholicism requires an understanding of some unbiblical aspects of the Catholic Church and a willingness to renounce these things. Various topics will be discussed followed by prayers related to the topics. In addition, the appendices offer web links to 103 Internet articles, 16 of which include pictures. They provide detailed information about the topics which are discussed here and will enable you to verify my information.

If you are involved in Catholicism and are seeking for answers, please consider praying the following prayer:

PRAYER: Heavenly Father, please open my heart and my mind to Your truth. Please help me respond to what I read according to Your will. Please set me free from the bondage of Catholicism. Please break its hold on my mind, my will, my emotions, my heart, my

conscience, my imagination, and my habits. In the name of Jesus. Amen.

1. UNGODLY POWER AND AUTHORITY

A. BECOMING ROMAN

The Christian Church was persecuted by the Roman Empire until 314 A.D. when Emperor Constantine made an alliance with the Church. At that time the Church became Roman in organization and approach. Church officials dressed and behaved like Roman noblemen. In 380 A.D., Emperor Theodosius required Roman subjects to accept Rome's version of Christianity. Pagans, Jews, and Christians who refused to comply were punished as heretics.

B. PAPAL CORRUPTION

Because Rome was an important city, the Bishop of Rome had prestige, power, and great possessions. Over the centuries, his power increased and his title changed from "Bishop of Rome" to "Pope." Papal wealth and power often motivated men to become Pope for the wrong reasons.

Some men bribed their way into the papacy. Some men became Pope by means of armies, mob violence, or murder. Once in power, popes gave lands and wealth to their family members. Some popes had mistresses or homosexual lovers. One pope had such a bad reputation for rape that pilgrims were afraid to come to Saint Peter's Cathedral. Some popes had dungeons and torturers.

Some popes were heretics and were denounced by Church Councils and by other popes. One pope sold some Italian peasants into slavery because he had a dispute with their masters. Two of the most corrupt popes were Pope John XII and Pope Alexander VI.

Pope John XII was a violent man. He was so lustful that people of his day said he turned the Lateran Palace into a brothel. He drank toasts to the devil. When gambling, he invoked pagan gods and goddesses. He was killed by a jealous husband while in the act of committing adultery with the man's wife.

Pope Alexander VI was known for murder, bribery, and selling positions of authority in the Church. He was grossly licentious. On one occasion, he required 50 prostitutes to dance naked before him and to engage in sexual acts for his entertainment. He had cardinals killed so that he could confiscate their property and sell their positions to ambitious men. He died of poison after having dinner with a cardinal. It was rumored that the cardinal suspected that the Pope would try to poison him so he switched wine goblets with the Pope.

C. INCREASING PAPAL POWER

Pope Gregory VII made cardinals, kings, and emperors kiss his foot. He used excommunication to force kings and emperors to obey him. Catholics believed that the Catholic Church and its sacraments were necessary to go to Heaven. Therefore excommunication was considered to be a sentence of damnation to hell. The only remedy was to submit to the Pope and beg him to repeal the sentence.

A number of forged documents were used by Gregory VII and his successors in order to expand the power of the papacy. Some Roman Catholics tried to expose these forgeries, but they were excommunicated for it. Orthodox Christians, however, were able to write detailed information about the forgeries.

Pope Innocent III declared the Pope to be ruler of the world and father of princes and kings. He claimed that every priest and bishop must obey the Pope, even if he commands something evil. He further stated that no one had a right to judge the Pope.

Pope Innocent III forced the King of France to kill hundreds of thousands of French citizens in order to get rid of the Albigensian heretics. Because the Albigensians lived mingled among the French Catholics, the Pope commanded that every person in the region, including the Catholics, be killed. This was called the Albigensian Crusade. The Pope gave the Albigensian Crusaders a special indulgence which was supposed to guarantee that if they died in battle, their sins would be remitted and they would go to Heaven.

D. THE INQUISITION

The Fourth Lateran Council was held in 1215 during the reign of Pope Innocent III. It decreed that heretics were to be turned over to secular authorities to be killed. Catholics who helped exterminate heretics were given the same indulgences and privileges as Crusaders.

Those who disagreed with any Catholic doctrine or any papal pronouncement were considered to be heretics. The Inquisition expanded the definition of heresy to include things like reading the Bible or eating meat during Lent. When the Spanish came to Latin America, they brought the Inquisition with them. Natives were tortured and killed for refusing to convert to Catholicism.

For six centuries the Inquisition tortured people who were accused of heresy. Many of them were sentenced to death. Others were imprisoned. Inquisitors required Catholics to report family members who said or did anything suspicious. Children were required to tell the Inquisitors if their parents did things such as reading a forbidden book or eating meat during Lent.

When people were accused of heresy, they were not allowed to know what the charges were or who their accusers were. They were tortured. If they confessed then they were usually sent to prison. If they refused to confess then the Inquisitors sentenced them to be killed by the civil authorities. If the civil authorities failed to cooperate, then the Inquisitors accused them of heresy. As a result, the civil authorities became victims of the system. The Inquisitors said that they would rather kill 100 innocent people than let one heretic go free.

The Catholic Church was able to technically keep its hands clean of bloodshed. The Inquisitors used methods of torture which caused intense pain but usually did not cause bleeding. According to the rules, the Inquisitors were not supposed to kill people. However, they tortured them severely, which in some cases would result in death due to shock, heart failure, and other stress-related causes. When the Inquisitors sentenced heretics to death, the local civil authorities did the actual killing (under threat of being condemned as heretics if they refused). Catholic apologists who say that relatively few people were killed by the Inquisition are technically correct because the Inquisitors themselves normally did not do the actual killing. However, Protestant historians and records kept by the Orthodox Church indicate that millions of people were killed as a result of the Inquisition.

When Inquisitors sentenced heretics to death, the sentence specified the means of execution. In Europe, heretics were often burned at the stake. In Latin America, other forms of execution were also used. Heretics could be impaled or slowly roasted above a fire.

When people were convicted of heresy, the Inquisitors took their money and their property. Inquisitors dug up dead men, convicted them of heresy, and took their property. This meant they were able to confiscate property which had been inherited by the families of the dead heretics.

E. THE CRUSADES

Popes had Crusades in order to take the Holy Land from the Muslims. Preachers were commissioned to inspire their followers to join the Crusades. The Pope gave indulgences to the Crusaders, promising that if they died while on the Crusade then their sins would be remitted and they would go to Heaven.

The Crusaders went through Europe on their way to the Holy Land. While going through Europe, they killed Jews and "heretics." When they reached the Holy Land, the Crusaders killed Orthodox Christians and desecrated Orthodox churches.

When the First Crusade conquered Jerusalem, there was massive slaughter. Six thousand Jews took refuge in a synagogue. The Crusaders set it on fire. While the Jews were being burned alive, the Crusaders rode around the synagogue singing hymns. Thirty thousand Muslims took refuge inside the Dome of the Rock (an important mosque) and were slaughtered there. The streets ran with so much blood that the horses splashed it onto the legs of their riders. One Crusader wrote that they rode in blood which came up to the knees of their horses. Some Crusaders dismembered the bodies of people who had been killed. They made piles of heads and hands and feet. In some places the streets were so full of bodies that it was difficult for the horses to find safe footing.

The Fourth Crusade conquered Constantinople instead of going to the Holy Land. Constantinople was the center of the Orthodox Church, the location of its ruler (the Patriarch) and its greatest cathedral (Hagia Sophia). The Crusaders killed the men, plundered the city and set many buildings on fire. They raped and murdered matrons, girls, and Orthodox nuns. They vandalized tombs of Orthodox emperors. They placed a notorious harlot in the seat of the Patriarch where she sang obscene songs and performed lewd dances. The Crusaders desecrated the Cathedral of Hagia Sophia. Consecrated bread and wine were thrown on the ground and trampled underfoot. Icons and religious objects of value were taken as booty. The altar was smashed and the pieces were taken as plunder. Reliquaries were broken open and the relics were treated disgracefully.

These things were done by people who called themselves Christians, under the banner of the cross, in the name of Jesus Christ. The Bible says, "For the name of God is blasphemed among the Gentiles through you, as it is written" (Romans 2:24).

The Jews and Muslims have not forgotten the Crusades. Some atheists, agnostics, Wiccans, and neo-pagans have Internet articles which claim that the Crusades and the Inquisition demonstrate the true nature of Christianity. The Inquisition and the Crusades have made it difficult for some people to believe the Gospel and receive salvation.

F. MORE PAPAL POWER

The claims of papal power continued increasing. In 1870, the Pope was declared to be infallible. The 1917 Code of Canon Law increased the power and authority of the Pope. In 1983, Pope

John Paul II revised the Code of Canon Law. He added new laws that further increased the legal basis for the power and authority of the Pope.

G. SUMMARY

The Roman Catholic Church is built on control, manipulation, violence, terror, lies, and fraud. Popes gained power through the use of forged documents, waging war, dethroning kings and emperors, threatening people with damnation, and persecuting Christians who disagreed with them. The Inquisition lasted for six centuries. It spread terror and bloodshed throughout the known world. The Crusades damaged the credibility of Christians in the eyes of other people.

> **PRAYER: Heavenly Father, I renounce every form of ungodly authority and ungodly power. I repent of every way in which I have abused my authority over someone else. I repent of submitting to ungodly authority. I repent of having been a member of a church which has a history of using terror, bloodshed, torture, lies, fraud, control, and manipulation. I repent of my loyalty to the popes. I declare that You are my spiritual authority and not any pope or priest. I renounce greed, control, manipulation, coercion, deception, sexual immorality, violence, and the lust for power. Please show me any ways in which I have participated in these things and give me the grace of heartfelt repentance. Please get these things out of my heart and out of my life. Please heal me from any harm I have**

suffered as a result of allowing other people do these things to me.   Please set me free from every form of control by the Catholic Church.   Please set me free from every ungodly influence of the Catholic Church. In the name of Jesus.   Amen.

2. OPPOSING THE BIBLE

There are many Catholic doctrines which are contrary to the Bible. What I have written here is for those who are already aware of this fact. If you want to know more about the contradictions, I recommend the book *The Gospel According to Rome* by James McCarthy (Harvest House Publishers). This book, written by a former Catholic, compares Catholic doctrine with the Bible. McCarthy thoroughly documents his findings by using official Catholic sources.

The Catholic Church teaches that Catholic tradition has as much authority as Scripture, and that only the Church can accurately interpret the Bible.   Catholics are not allowed to let the Bible speak for itself. They are required to find out how the Catholic Church interprets it. They are required to filter what they read in the Bible through the lenses of Catholic doctrines. For example, the Bible speaks of "James the Lord's brother" (Galatians 1:19). It gives the names of four men who were Jesus' brothers, and it mentions that He also had sisters (Matthew 13:53-57; Mark 6:1-4). But Catholics must read these passages without ever questioning the doctrine that Mary was always a virgin.

For centuries, the Catholic Church kept the Bible in Latin, which most people could not understand. Men who translated the Bible into English were killed as heretics. The Council of Trent declared that only certain special people were allowed to read the Bible. As a result, many men and women were killed as heretics for nothing more than reading the Bible.

> **PRAYER: Heavenly Father, I repent for believing in a church which tries to keep people from understanding the Bible for themselves. I renounce everything which has been done to put barriers between people and the Bible. Please help me understand the Bible, trust it, and apply it to my life in practical ways. Please make me hungry for Your truth. Please help me know You, Your character, and Your ways of dealing with Your people. Please help me to love You and trust You. In the name of Jesus. Amen.**

3. PAGAN PRACTICES

Following are some specific examples showing how Catholicism is actually based on pagan religious practices.

A. RITUALS

The Catholic Church teaches that if a Catholic priest says the correct words and performs the correct ritual actions then bread and wine will literally turn into the body, blood, soul, and divinity of Jesus Christ. This is both magic and idolatry. The Eucharist is an idol made by human hands and human words. When Catholics worship the Eucharist, their love and gratitude goes to a piece of bread instead of going to Jesus Christ.

B. REPETITIOUS PRAYERS

Catholic Mass consists largely of standard written prayers and responses which are repeated at every Mass. However, there is some variety due to Scripture readings, the homily, and special prayers in honor of Mary, saints, and holy days.

The rosary is a series of repeated prayers with ten "Hail Marys" for every "Our Father." Although some pray the rosary slowly and thoughtfully, others say the prayers rapidly and automatically. Sometimes people say the prayers so rapidly that the words are indistinguishable. But the Bible says, "But when ye pray, use not vain repetitions, as the heathen do; for they think that they shall be heard for their much speaking" (Matthew 6:7).

C. COMMUNICATING WITH THE DEAD

Catholics are taught to pray to Mary and the saints. These are dead people. But the Bible says that we should seek help from God; we should not seek the help of the dead on behalf of the living (see Isaiah 8:19).

Jesus Christ is alive. He was resurrected from the dead. When we pray to Jesus, we are praying to someone who is alive. The Bible says, "For therefore we both labour and suffer reproach, because we trust in the **living God**, who is the Saviour of all men, specially of those that believe" (1 Timothy 4:10, emphasis added). Paul and Barnabus told the people of Lystra, "We also are men of like passions with you, and preach unto you that ye should turn from these vanities unto the **living God**, which made heaven, and earth, and the sea, and all things that are therein" (Acts 14:15, emphasis added).

D. SACRED OBJECTS

Webster's Dictionary defines a charm as "anything worn to avert ill or secure good fortune." Charms are actually idols because people attribute power to them. People put their trust in the charms instead of relying on God.

Holy water is said to bring blessings and protection. There are other objects which are thought to be powerful, including holy oil, blessed salt, relics, statues, pictures, and crucifixes. Some people use the sign of the cross in a superstitious way when they are afraid. These are all ways of trusting in material things instead of trusting Jesus Christ. It is worshiping created things instead of worshiping the Creator. It is similar to the pagan use of charms and talismans.

The rosary, the brown scapular, and special devotions to Mary are said to help people get to Heaven. Special medals, scapulars, pictures, statues, and candles are said to bring blessings. Novenas and other special prayers are said to cause people to get what they want. Lourdes water, Saint Anne's oil, the Saint Benedict medal, some relics, and other objects are said to cause physical healing. These are like the charms and incantations of pagan religions or witchcraft. True Christians trust in Jesus Christ, not in material objects, special words, and rituals.

E. PAINFUL PRACTICES

Some Catholics believe that they will receive favors from God or from saints if they do painful things such as whipping themselves or walking on their knees. This is similar to pagan religions in which followers are required to do painful things in order to gain favors from their gods.

F. SUMMARY

Christian prayer is approaching God with our needs in a spirit of humility, and trusting that God loves us and He will do what is best for us. Attempts to make things happen by using special objects, special words, or special rituals are actually attempts to supernaturally take control. This is similar to witchcraft or magic or sorcery. God calls these things an abomination and He warned His people not to do them. (See Exodus 22:18; Deuteronomy 18:9-12.)

> **PRAYER: Heavenly Father, I repent of trusting in rituals and objects instead of trusting in Your love for me. I repent of attributing power to rituals and objects instead of believing in Your power, Your love, and Your faithfulness. I repent of praying to dead people. I renounce every form of magic, sorcery, fortune telling, divination, witchcraft, and communication with the dead. Please set me free from every influence of these things in my life. If I ever start to do anything superstitious or magical, please convict me and give me the grace for heartfelt repentance. Please get these things out of my heart and out of my life. Please set me free from any influence of paganism or the occult. Please set me free from any spiritual or emotional harm that was caused by these things. Please increase my faith and my trust in You. In the name of Jesus. Amen.**

4. UNBIBLICAL PRAYERS

There are special prayers which come from saints who had mystical experiences, visions, or apparitions. Some of these prayers involve the repetitious use of special verbal formulas. Some of them are associated with special medals, pictures, or other objects.

Biblical prayer is not based on special words or objects. Biblical prayer is based on our faith in God and our personal relationship with Him. It is a natural form of communication, like talking with a close friend. The Psalms show how David poured out his heart to God. The New Testament shows how Jesus and the apostles prayed. They spoke from their hearts instead of using techniques and formulas. Three examples follow.

1. "For this cause I bow my knees unto the Father of our Lord Jesus Christ, Of whom the whole family in heaven and earth is named, That he would grant you, according to the riches of his glory, to be strengthened with might by his Spirit in the inner man; That Christ may dwell in your hearts by faith; that ye, being rooted and grounded in love, May be able to comprehend with all saints what is the breadth, and length, and depth, and height; And to know the love of Christ, which passeth knowledge, that ye might be filled with all the fulness of God" (Ephesians 3:14-19).

2. "For this cause we also, since the day we heard it, do not cease to pray for you, and to desire that ye might be filled with the knowledge of his will in all wisdom and spiritual understanding; That ye might walk worthy of the Lord

unto all pleasing, being fruitful in every good work, and increasing in the knowledge of God; Strengthened with all might, according to his glorious power, unto all patience and long-suffering with joyfulness; Giving thanks unto the Father, which hath made us meet to be partakers of the inheritance of the saints in light" (Colossians 1:9-12).

3. "Lord, thou art God, which hast made heaven, and earth, and the sea, and all that in them is: Who by the mouth of thy servant David hast said, Why did the heathen rage, and the people imagine vain things? The kings of the earth stood up, and the rulers were gathered together against the Lord, and against his Christ. For of a truth against thy holy child Jesus, whom thou has anointed, both Herod, and Pontius Pilate, with the Gentiles, and the people of Israel, were gathered together, For to do whatsoever thy hand and thy counsel determined before to be done. And now, Lord, behold their threatenings: and grant unto thy servants, that with all boldness they may speak thy word, By stretching forth thine hand to heal; and that signs and wonders may be done by the name of thy holy child Jesus" (Acts 4:24-30).

PRAYER: Heavenly Father, I renounce the repetition of special verbal formulas and the use of special objects. I repent for every way in which I have participated in such things. Please teach me how to pray with faith in Your love for me. Please teach me how to share my heart with You like a trusting child. In the name of Jesus. Amen.

5. IDOLATRY

The Catholic Church is built on idolatry, which is defined as the religious worship of an image, material object, or person. Instances of idolatry in Catholicism are:

A. THE CATHOLIC CHURCH

The Catholic Church itself is an idol. It claims that no one can get to Heaven without it and its sacraments. It claims to be infallible. It calls itself "Holy Mother Church." It demands absolute loyalty and obedience. When people believe what the Bible says instead of believing what the Catholic Church says, they are called heretics. Popes as recent as Pope Paul VI (who reigned from 1963 to 1978) have declared that there is no salvation apart from the Catholic Church.

B. THE POPE

The Pope is an idol. He claims to be infallible. He is called "Holy Father" and "Your Holiness." He is called the "Vicar of Christ." He demands loyalty and obedience. The Inquisition tortured people and had them killed for disagreeing with the Pope.

As was just stated, Popes have claimed that there is no salvation apart from the Pope. However, the Bible (speaking of Jesus) says, "Neither is there salvation in any other: for there is none other name under heaven given among men, whereby we must be saved" (Acts 4:12). Christian salvation comes by faith in Jesus Christ, not by faith in popes. We are saved in the name of Jesus, not the name of a Pope.

Several popes have made idolatrous statements of themselves. Pope Leo XIII said in 1894 that as Pope, he held on the earth the place of God Almighty. Pope Pius X ruled from 1903 to 1914. He is a canonized saint. He said that when the Pope speaks, it is Jesus Christ Himself speaking. Pope Pius XI reigned from 1922 to 1939. He said that because he was the Vicar of Christ he was "God on earth."

C. THE EUCHARIST

The Catholic Church says that during Mass the bread and wine literally turn into the body, blood, soul, and divinity of Jesus Christ. Catholics are taught to bow before the bread and to worship it. According to Catholic Canon Law, Catholics are supposed to worship the Eucharist with "supreme adoration" (Canon 898).

D. MARY AND THE SAINTS

Catholics pray to Mary and to saints. These are idols. Jesus is the only Savior. He is the only Mediator. He is the one who prays to the Father for us. Mary and the saints died long ago. Dead people cannot help us.

The Bible says, "Verily I say unto you, Among them that are born of women there hath not risen a greater than John the Baptist" (Matthew 11:11). This statement by Jesus indicates that not even Mary was greater than John the Baptist. Jesus did not elevate Mary above others. On the contrary, He publicly corrected her (Matthew 12:46-50; Luke 2:48-50; John 2:3-4). In spite of this, some popes have said that we have to go through Mary in order to get to Jesus.

Catholic Canon Law says that all Catholics should cultivate devotion to Mary, including praying the rosary (Canon 663, Section 4). Furthermore, every fixed altar in churches is required to have a relic of a saint (Canon 1237, Section 2).

E. STATUES

Some Catholic statues are treated like pagan idols. There are statues of Mary which wear expensive clothing decorated with gold and jewels. Some of them wear crowns made of real gold, some of which are adorned with jewels. There is an official Catholic ritual for crowning statues of Mary. There are photographs of the Pope bowing before a statue of Mary and kissing its feet.

There is a bronze statue of the Apostle Peter in the Vatican. On the feast day for Saint Peter, the statue is clothed with regal garments and crowned with a gold papal tiara. Some Catholics light votive candles in front of statues or kneel in front of statues to pray.

Statues of Mary and saints are often carried through city streets in processions. Some of these processions are quite large. In October 1999, a procession of two and a half million Catholics followed a statue of the Virgin of Zapopan. In December 2001, more than eight million Catholics came to Mexico City to honor Our Lady of Guadalupe, including huge processions following a painting of the apparition. In Fatima, Portugal, it is traditional to have candlelight processions in honor of Our Lady of Fatima. Crowds of pilgrims carrying lighted candles follow a statue. Sometimes these processions have a million people.

The Infant of Prague is a statue of Jesus as a baby. It is in a church in Prague, Czechoslovakia. Miracles are attributed to this statue. Pilgrims come from around the world to venerate it. The statue wears expensive clothing and a gold crown set with jewels. It has 70 different sets of clothes. In 1995, the statue was carried in solemn procession through the streets of Prague. The procession was led by two cardinals. Churches in many countries have replicas of this highly venerated statue.

Catholic Canon Law says that Catholic churches should have "holy images" (statues, pictures, mosaics, etc.) and that Catholics should venerate these images (Canons 1186-1190). However, the Bible forbids the veneration of statues or other images. It says "Thou shalt not make thee any graven image, or any likeness of any thing that is in heaven above, or that is in the earth beneath, or that is in the waters beneath the earth: Thou shalt not bow down thyself unto them, nor serve them" (Deuteronomy 5:8-9).

PRAYER: Heavenly Father, I renounce every form of idolatry. I repent for every way in which I have participated in idolatry. Only You are holy. Only You can save me. Only You are worthy of worship. Please remove all idolatry from my heart, my mind, and my life. If I start to do anything idolatrous, please show me and give me the grace for heartfelt repentance. Please help me worship You with all of my heart, with all of my mind, with all of my strength, with all of my soul, and with all of my loyalty. Please teach me to worship You in spirit and in truth. In the name of Jesus. Amen.

6. APPARITIONS OF "MARY"

Something supernatural has been appearing to people. It claims to be the Virgin Mary. It draws people away from Jesus and towards Mary. It encourages people to pray rosaries, wear scapulars, and consecrate themselves to Mary. It claims that Mary can get people into Heaven.

Sometimes "Mary" appears with "baby Jesus" in her arms. However, Jesus is not a baby. He was a grown man when He was crucified, resurrected from the dead, and ascended into Heaven. Jesus was a grown man in resurrected glory when Stephen was being stoned and he saw the heavens opened and Jesus standing at the right hand of God the Father (Acts 7:55-56). When Jesus returns in glory at the Second Coming, He will not return as a baby. On Judgment Day, the human race will not be judged by a baby.

The Bible warns us that the devil can appear as an angel of light (see 2 Corinthians 11:14). Therefore, we should not be surprised if the devil and his demons can appear in the form of the Virgin Mary. The Bible warns us that there will be lying signs and wonders whose purpose is to deceive people and draw them away from God (see Matthew 24:24; 2 Thessalonians 2:9-10).

PRAYER: Heavenly Father, I renounce every kind of devotion to the Virgin Mary. I renounce the veneration of Mary. I renounce worship of Mary. I renounce every special title which has been given to Mary. I renounce belief in apparitions of "Mary." I renounce everything that I have said or done because of instructions from these apparitions. I repent of everything

that I have said or done in order to venerate the Virgin Mary or to show special devotion to her.   I repent of any way in which I have consecrated myself to Mary. I repent of praying the Rosary. I repent of wearing medals, jewelry, rosary bracelets, or scapulars that honor Mary. I repent of saying prayers to Mary and singing songs in her honor. I repent of asking Mary to intervene on my behalf instead of trusting You to hear my prayers because You love me. I repent of believing that Mary could help me or my loved ones.   I repent of ever saying or implying that the Virgin Mary is my queen or my mother. I declare that Mary was an ordinary woman who was given the privilege of being the mother of Jesus. She made mistakes like the rest of us. She needed a savior like the rest of us. Please forgive me for believing Catholic doctrines which exalt Mary above other people. Please forgive me for making an idol out of her. In the name of Jesus. Amen.

7. FALSE THEOLOGY

Thomas Aquinas was one of the most influential Catholic theologians that lived. His experiences and philosophies heavily influenced his writing. He trusted forged documents which gave him a false picture of Church history. He was also strongly influenced by Greek philosophers, especially Aristotle. He had mystical experiences, including an apparition of "Mary" which spoke to him.

According to the *Catholic Encyclopedia*, Thomas Aquinas had "ecstasies" (an "ecstasy" is an altered state of consciousness associated with special spiritual experiences of mystics). He saw an apparition of angels and an apparition of "Mary." He also heard a voice speak to him from the crucifix on the altar. In 1273, he had an ecstasy which caused him to stop writing. He said that what he had written before now seemed to him to be of little value. He then prepared to die.

PRAYER: Heavenly Father, I renounce every false doctrine. I repent for believing them. Please uproot them from my heart and from my mind. Please open my eyes to the truth of the Bible and set me free from every false teaching. I renounce pagan philosophy. I renounce every form of fraud, lies, and false history. I renounce ungodly mystical experiences. I renounce doctrines and information which come from apparitions of "Mary." I renounce every ungodly belief which comes from these things. Please give me a renewed mind and a renewed heart. When I hear false teaching, please help me recognize that it is false. Please protect me from every form of deception. In the name of Jesus. Amen.

8. GREED

The Catholic Church is built on greed. Popes sold positions of power and authority in the Catholic Church. Men could become bishops, abbots, or cardinals if they paid the Pope enough money for it. One Pope was so greedy that he had cardinals killed so that he could sell their positions to other men. Rich men paid

Catholic clergy to forgive their sins. Church officials sold dispensations. For a payment, a man or woman could be dispensed from Church requirements such as fasting during Lent. The Bible says, "For the love of money is the root of all evil: which while some coveted after, they have erred from the faith, and pierced themselves through with many sorrows" (1 Timothy 6:10).

The Catholic Church teaches that in order to get to Heaven, most people must first go to Purgatory where they suffer for their sins and are purified so that they can go to Heaven. Popes said that they were able to get people out of Purgatory and into Heaven. The means for accomplishing this was indulgences, which people could purchase. Preachers were given the assignment of selling indulgences. They spoke of the horrible torments of Purgatory. They then told people that when they bought an indulgence for a deceased loved one, the soul of their loved one immediately escaped from Purgatory and went to Heaven. People also believed that buying an indulgence for themselves guaranteed that their sins would be forgiven, including sins committed after the purchase of the indulgence. This encouraged people to sin without fear of spiritual consequences.

PRAYER: Heavenly Father, I renounce every form of greed. I renounce every kind of evil that results from the lust for money. I repent of having been a member of a church that deceived people in order to get money from them. Please help me trust You to provide for my needs and the needs of my loved ones. Please help me have righteous behavior and right motives when dealing with money and property. In the name of Jesus. Amen.

9. MISDIRECTED LOYALTY

The Catholic Church is built on misdirected loyalty. Catholics give to the Catholic Church the faith, trust, love, loyalty, and gratitude which should be given to Jesus Christ. Catholics often have strong emotional ties to the Catholic Church. These need to be broken so that people will be free to believe and obey the Bible and to love and serve God according to the principles given in the Bible.

> **PRAYER: Heavenly Father, I renounce every form of false loyalty. My primary loyalty belongs to You and to You alone. I repent for giving the Catholic Church the love, trust, loyalty, and gratitude which I should have given to you. I repent for every way in which I have put other things ahead of You. Please help me put You first all of the time. Please help me see things from Your perspective. In the name of Jesus. Amen.**

10. FORBIDDEN MARRIAGES

Peter was married. We know this because Jesus healed Peter's mother-in-law of a fever (see Matthew 8:14-15; Mark 1:30-31; Luke 4:38-39). Some of the Apostles were married. The Apostle Paul said "Have we not power to lead about a sister, a wife, as well as other apostles, and as the brethren of the Lord, and Cephas [Peter]?" (1 Corinthians 9:5).

In the early Church, many priests were married. Some Popes decided that they would have more power if the priests were not married, so they decreed laws forbidding priests to get married. One result was widespread sexual immorality. Many Catholic clergy went to prostitutes, had mistresses, or had homosexual lovers. Some priests seduced or raped women when they went to confession. Some priests got nuns pregnant and then killed the babies. The laws against marriage resulted in sexual immorality, perversion, seduction, rape, hypocrisy, injustice, cruelty, and murder.

Peter de Rosa used to be a priest. He is a practicing Catholic who did research in the Vatican Archives while he was a priest. His book *Vicars of Christ* gives extensive quotations from official Catholic Church documents that describe the sexual immorality of Catholic clergy during various periods of church history. This is still going on today. There are numerous modern instances of priests raping and otherwise sexually exploiting children, adolescents, and nuns.

PRAYER: Heavenly Father, I renounce every form of sexual immorality, perversion, seduction, rape, killing babies, and hypocrisy. I repent of being part of a church which allowed priests to engage in these activities for hundreds of years. I repent of every sexual sin which I have committed in thought, word, deed, or imagination. Please enable me to be faithful to You and to resist every form of sexual sin. Please give me a pure heart. In the name of Jesus. Amen.

11. FORBIDDEN FOODS

The Catholic Church required abstinence from eating meat during Lent and on certain special days. In some countries, Catholics also had to abstain from eating any animal products during Lent, including milk, butter, cheese, and eggs. People who broke the rules were accused of heresy. During the Inquisition, many were tortured and killed for eating meat or eggs or drinking milk during Lent.

Until the Second Vatican Council (1962-1965), it was considered to be a mortal sin for Catholics to eat meat on Fridays. After Vatican II, the fasting rules were relaxed. Most modern Catholics believe that they only need to abstain from eating meat on Ash Wednesday and on Fridays during Lent. However, Canon Law still says that bishops are supposed to require Catholics to abstain from eating meat or some other food every single Friday. In 1997, the Catholic bishops of America met to discuss whether or not they should require Catholics to abstain from eating meat on all Fridays.

Fasting is scriptural, but it should be a matter of personal conviction and not external compulsion. The Bible says that Christians should not judge one another based on what they eat or drink (see Colossians 2:16).

PRAYER: Heavenly Father, I repent of serving a church that required people to fast and that killed people for eating meat during Lent. I renounce every form of coercion. I declare that all people should have freedom of conscience. I thank you for giving

us free will. I repent for every way in which I have tried to violate the free will of others. Please help me respect and protect the free will that You have graciously given to me and to all people. In the name of Jesus. Amen.

12. DOCTRINES OF DEMONS

The Bible says, "Now the Spirit speaketh expressly, that in the latter times some shall depart from the faith, giving heed to seducing spirits, and doctrines of devils; Speaking lies in hypocrisy; having their conscience seared with a hot iron; **Forbidding to marry, and commanding to abstain from meats**, which God hath created to be received with thanksgiving of them which believe and know the truth" (1 Timothy 4:1-3, emphasis added). The Bible connects the doctrines of demons with a combination of two things: (1) forbidding marriage, and (2) forbidding people to eat certain foods.

Catholic doctrine led to the conclusion that people should be tortured and killed for eating meat during Lent. This doctrine is totally contrary to the teaching and example of Jesus Christ. It is a demonstration that the Catholic Church has been listening to deceiving spirits and teaching doctrines of demons. Other Catholic doctrines of demons include papal infallibility, Purgatory, and doctrines which promote veneration of the Virgin Mary.

Some Catholic doctrines are true teachings from the Bible, such as Jesus Christ died to save us from our sins and He was resurrected from the dead. The Bible tells us to test every teaching and every doctrine by comparing it with what the Bible says. Here are three specific references:

1. "And the brethren immediately sent away Paul and Silas by night unto Berea: who coming thither went into the synagogue of the Jews. These were more noble than those in Thessalonica, in that they received the word with all readiness of mind, and **searched the scriptures daily, whether those things were so**" (Acts 17:10-11, emphasis added).

2. "Beloved, believe not every spirit, but try the spirits whether they are of God: because many false prophets are gone out into the world" (1 John 4:1).

3. "All scripture is given by inspiration of God, and is profitable for doctrine, for reproof, for correction, for instruction in righteousness; That the man of God may be perfect, thoroughly furnished unto all good works" (2 Timothy 3:16-17).

PRAYER: Heavenly Father, I renounce every doctrine which comes from demons. I repent of having believed them. I repent of having agreed with the devil. I declare that the Roman Catholic Church teaches doctrines of demons but it also teaches some true things which come from the Bible. Please help me recognize the difference between them. Help me know what is true and what is false. Please give me clear discernment. Please enable me to recognize whether or not teachings are consistent with the Bible and with Your nature and character. In the name of Jesus. Amen.

13. SAINTS

The Bible does not talk about a special class of especially holy people who are called saints. In the New Testament, every Christian believer is called a saint. The Catholic Church has a special group of people which it calls saints. This is wrong for several reasons:

1. Only God has the authority and the wisdom to correctly judge people.

2. The Bible says that God does not have special favorites. He listens to the prayers of everybody who loves Him.

3. To elevate a group of Christians above all other Christians is a form of idolatry.

4. The Bible calls all Christians saints (see Acts 9:13,32,41; 26:10; Romans 1:7; 8:27; 12:13; 15:25,26,31; 16:2,15; 1 Corinthians 1:2; 6:1,2; 14:33; 16:1,15; 2 Corinthians 1:1; 8:4; 9:1,12; 13:13; Ephesians 1:1,15,18; 2:19; 3:8,18; 4:12; 5:3; 6:18; Philippians 1:1; 4:22; Colossians 1:2,4,12,26; 1 Thessalonians 3:13; 2 Thessalonians 1:10; 1 Timothy 5:10; Philemon 1:5,7; Hebrews 6:10; 13:24; Jude 1:3,14).

If you were named after a saint or were given a saint's name at confirmation, then you need to renounce your connection with that saint. If you have a patron saint, then you need to renounce your connection with that saint and repent of having turned to that saint with your needs instead of turning directly to God.

Jesus told us that God is our Father. Children have direct access to their fathers. They don't need to approach them through intermediaries. Our Heavenly Father hears our prayers because He loves us and because we are His children.

> **PRAYER: Heavenly Father, I renounce any connection that I have had with any Catholic saint. I repent of being influenced by their penances and mystical experiences. I repent of everything I did to honor any saint. I repent for asking saints to pray for me. Please remove any harmful influence that saints have had in my life. Please set me free from any confusion which saints have caused. I want my life to be based on Your truth which You have revealed in the Bible. In the name of Jesus. Amen.**

14. UNCLEAN OBJECTS

The Bible tells us that objects which are used for idolatry or other pagan practices are an abomination to God. They are accursed objects and they will bring a curse on anyone who owns them. If you have any of these objects then you need to destroy them or get rid of them.

The Bible says, "The graven images of their gods shall ye burn with fire: thou shalt not desire the silver or gold that is on them, nor take it unto thee, lest thou be snared therein: for it is an abomination to the Lord thy God. **Neither shalt thou bring an abomination into thine house, lest thou be a cursed thing like it**: but thou shalt utterly detest it, and thou shalt utterly abhor it; for it is a cursed thing" (Deuteronomy 7:25-26, emphasis added).

Such objects include rosaries, chaplets, and other religious objects which are associated with saying special prayers. They also include medals, scapulars, rosary bracelets, religious jewelry, and other religious objects which are associated with devotion to Mary or saints. They include relics. They include holy water and other things which are supposed to bring blessing or protection. They include statues, pictures, holy cards, or jewelry of Mary, the saints, and Michael the Archangel. They include pictures and holy cards of the Pope and other objects which honor the Catholic Church. They include objects associated with visions or mystical experiences of saints. They include anything related to apparitions of "Mary."

You need to get rid of any object which is said to bring good luck or provide protection. God is our protector, not objects. You need to get rid of anything which is related to witchcraft, spiritism, fortune telling, divination, contacting the dead, astrology, or pagan religions.

God may show you other things you need to get rid of. If you aren't sure whether or not you should get rid of something, then ask God to show you. If you still aren't sure, then the safe thing is to get rid of it.

If something has sentimental value, then ask God to help you get rid of it in spite of your attachment to it. If getting rid of an object might hurt somebody's feelings, then ask God to show you ways to reassure the person of your love and appreciation. Do not allow someone's feelings to prevent you from getting rid of the object. What God thinks about you is far more important than what any person thinks about you.

PRAYER: Heavenly Father, I am willing to get rid of any object that is associated with idolatry, paganism,

witchcraft, spiritism, magic, or other false religious practices. Please make me aware of these objects and help me get rid of them. If any curse has come upon me, please set me free from the curse and replace it with Your blessings. Please set me free from every spiritual or emotional tie to the Catholic Church or to any other false religion. Please set me free from any kind of demonic influence or bondage. Thank You that You are faithful, You love me, and You are all powerful. You are my protector and my deliverer. You have promised to make everything work out for my good because I love You. Please increase my confidence in Your love for me and Your ability to take good care of me. In the name of Jesus. Amen.

15. MIXING PAGANISM WITH CHRISTIANITY

Saint Peter's Basilica in Rome is a visual representation of the true nature of the Roman Catholic Church. It is huge, impressive, expensive, ornate, and full of beautiful artwork. It is a place where popes and cardinals participate in elaborate rituals. It is built on top of an ancient Roman graveyard which is called a necropolis, a city of the dead. Saint Peter's is built on dead men's bones and tombs with artwork depicting pagan gods. The location is a place of death and pagan religion.

The site of Saint Peter's was originally the location of the Circus of Nero (the Circus Maximus) where Christians were martyred. It was a place of cruelty, bloodshed, and the painful death of many Christians. The circus shows often ended with a mockery of the crucifixion of Christ. The great obelisk from the Circus Maximus was moved to the square in front of Saint Peter's. Obelisks are associated with pagan religions. This particular obelisk was also associated with the brutal murder of Christians for public entertainment.

On the ceiling of the Sistine Chapel are painted God, Adam and Eve, patriarchs, prophets, apostles, pagan philosophers, and pagan prophetesses. It is a mixture of Christianity, pagan philosophy, and pagan religion.

PRAYER: Heavenly Father, I repent of being part of a church which mixes paganism with Christianity. I renounce all pagan beliefs and practices. Please set me free from every pagan influence in my mind, my heart, my imagination, and my habits. In the name of Jesus. Amen.

16. FORGIVING

Jesus told us to forgive one another. He said, "For if ye forgive men their trespasses, your heavenly Father will also forgive you: But if ye forgive not men their trespasses, neither will your Father forgive your trespasses" (Matthew 6:14-15). The Bible also says, "Follow peace with all men, and holiness, without which no man shall see the Lord: Looking diligently lest any man fail of the grace of God; lest any root of bitterness springing up trouble you, and thereby many be defiled" (Hebrews 12:14-15).

It can be difficult to forgive those who taught us false doctrines and ungodly religious practices. However you don't have to do it alone. God will help you. "The things which are impossible with men are possible with God" (Luke 18:27). If you are willing to forgive, then God will enable you to do it.

PRAYER: Heavenly Father, I choose to forgive every person who taught me false doctrines or ungodly religious practices. I also choose to forgive myself for allowing myself to believe false doctrines and to participate in ungodly religious practices. Please work in my heart so that I will completely forgive these people. Please give me Your love for them. Please work in their hearts and set them free from deception. In the name of Jesus. Amen.

17. FREEDOM FROM BONDAGE

Our faith is in Jesus Christ, not in the Catholic Church. Our source of authority is the Bible, not priests or popes or Catholic doctrines. We are saved by our faith in Jesus Christ, not by sacraments or good works or the Catholic Church. Our love and gratitude belong to God, not to the Catholic Church.

Sometimes Catholic friends and family members put pressure on former Catholics to return to Catholicism. If that happens to you, then you will need to stand your ground. Do not allow pressure from others to cause you to return to the bondage of Catholicism. The Bible says, "Stand fast therefore in the liberty where-with Christ hath made us free, and be not entangled again with the yoke of bondage" (Galatians 5:1).

> **PRAYER: Heavenly Father, thank You for setting me free from every form of bondage to the Catholic Church. Please help me live according to the freedom which You have given me. Please help me grow into a strong, mature Christian. Please increase my faith in You, my trust in You, and my loyalty to You. Help me truly believe in Your goodness, Your faithfulness, and Your mercy. Please help me understand how much You love me. Please help me respond with love, grati-tude, and faithfulness. I want my life to glorify You. I want to demonstrate Your love and Your character. In the name of Jesus. Amen.**

Recovering from Catholicism is a process that requires time and prayer. Sometimes it involves fear, doubt, grief, or anger. God will help you. He is faithful, He is able to help you, and He loves you. God's grace is sufficient to get you through it. He told the Apostle Paul, "My grace is sufficient for thee: for my strength is made perfect in weakness" (2 Corinthians 12:9).

You need to find a good Christian church which believes the Bible; a church where you can grow as a Christian. You need to read the Bible, asking God to help you understand it.

If you know others who are former Catholics, then you can help one another. You can befriend one another and become prayer partners. You can get together to pray for one another, encourage one another, and provide a kind of understanding which those who have never been Catholic are usually unable to provide. The Bible says, "And if one prevails against him, two shall withstand him; and a threefold cord is not quickly broken" (Ecclesiastes 4:12).

If your friends disagree with you about some things, remember that you are there to build one another up, not to argue. The Bible says that Christians should avoid unnecessary disputes because they generate strife (see 2 Timothy 2:23-24). It says, "Wherefore comfort yourselves together, and edify one another, even as also ye do" (1 Thessalonians 5:11). It also says, "Let us consider one another to provoke unto love and to good works: Not forsaking the assembling of ourselves together, as the manner of some is; but exhorting one another" (Hebrews 10:23-24).

"Now unto him that is able to keep you from falling, and to present you faultless before the presence of his glory with exceeding joy, To the only wise God our Saviour, be glory and majesty, dominion and power, both now and ever. Amen" (Jude 1:24).

AFTERWORD

by
CHUCK D. PIERCE

Second Thessalonians 2:3 says, "Don't let anyone deceive you in any way, for that day will not come until the rebellion occurs and the man of lawlessness is revealed, the man doomed to destruction." What this says is that there will be a remnant group alive at the Lord's coming who will have seen the Antichrist. We will understand His workings fully before we see Jesus face to face.

THE ROMAN CATHOLIC CHURCH: THE ONLY CHURCH?

As we move into this next season of history in the church, we are seeing a major contrast between false religions and the reality of God. It is similar to what we read about in the New Testament when Jesus was constantly at conflict with the Sadducees and Pharisees. We will also see political systems aligning with these religious groups in days ahead. This will produce a new dimension of the antichrist system working in the earth. These politically-powered religious systems will establish themselves against a freedom and movement of God's Spirit on earth.

As an example of the increasing contrast between religion and reality, we need go no further than the unexpected official "note" by Cardinal Joseph Ratzinger, prefect of the Vatican's Congregation for the Doctrine of the Faith, issued September 5, 2000. The "note" has been regarded by ecumenists as a severe setback to the process of nurturing Catholic-Protestant relationships begun by Pope John XXIII in the Second Vatican Council of the 1960s. The decree, approved by Pope John Paul II, is "authoritative and binding" for Catholic bishops. It prohibits bishops from referring to Protestant churches as "sister churches" as many have been doing for three decades, because "the one, holy, Catholic, and apostolic Universal Church [i.e., the Roman Catholic Church—ed.] is not sister but 'mother' of all the particular Churches."

The idea that the only truly valid church on the face of the earth is the Roman Catholic Church is far from reality. It is the spirit of religion that has affirmed itself in a last-ditch attempt to deceive multitudes and to divert them from true faith in the only head of the church, who is Jesus Christ. As the war intensifies, we can expect this kind of religious deception to become increasingly more common and more intense.

THE HANDSHAKE BETWEEN SECTARIAN AND RELIGIOUS SPIRITS

Have you ever noticed how sectarian spirits work? They work with religious spirits to align with the political structure of a particular religious group in an effort to ostracize everyone else. Oftentimes an existing religious group will reject new revelation by God, and the one He chose to bring it forth. If that individual then bring the new revelation to another group that does accept it, then the first religious structure is likely to reject that whole group and ostracize them as well.

Religious spirits focus us on legalistic rules and regulations to the extent that we miss the overall picture of what God is doing. We can get so busy dotting every "i" and crossing every "t" that we miss the gist of the sentence. Jesus came to fulfill the law and the prophets. He did it through love. Faith works by love and faith overcomes. But when we are legalistic, we begin to weaken true faith and fall into criticism and judgmentalism rather than walking in the love of Christ.

This behavior is an opening for religious spirits to operate in our midst, and keep us focused on what everyone else is doing wrong rather than the Great Commission. May we all stay focused on the harvest field of the future and all that is necessary to bring it in, rather than on what's wrong with how someone else is doing it. *Behind all aspects of false religion are demonic powers and principalities. The Spirit of God can infiltrate the strong militant stronghold that has captured many individuals and held them through a false type of worship.*

"Then He charged them, saying, 'Take heed, beware of the leaven of the Pharisees and the leaven of Herod'" (Mark 8:15). When our spiritual communion becomes religious (that is, controlled by mandated methods and monitored by ordinances), we are in great danger of losing our relationship with a Holy God and His indwelling Spirit in the earth. Our intimate communion should bring us to know God, and better understand His plan for us in our destined time on earth. Our spiritual life should be aligned with God's Kingdom purposes and not our own or the earthly political desires of people. That is why Jesus told us to beware of the leaven of the Pharisees. Religion blinds. When religion enters into leadership, great opposition arises toward God's Kingdom purposes.

Furthermore, no amount of demonstration of supernatural power and insight can convince a religious structure to let go of its subjects. We see examples of this all the way through the Bible beginning with Pharaoh and culminating in the crucifixion of the Lord Jesus Christ. Even after the death of the firstborn in Egypt and losing the grip on God's covenant people, Pharaoh could not shake loose of his philosophy of control and mustered an army to recapture God's people.

Jesus demonstrated God's power in healings, signs, and deliverances. He even raised some from the dead and overcame death Himself. Yet, the Pharisees never believed. Religion had corrupted their ability to perceive God's redemptive plan in the earth. When religion aligns with the political structure of the time, it becomes even more powerful to rule and stop a true Kingdom perspective from entering God's creation on earth.

Life is movement. That is why Jesus was telling us to beware of religious and political spirits that can stop the movement of life. The analogy of leaven represents the principle that one small amount of leaven can corrupt the whole batch. The deadly power of a religious spirit can enter any religious structure on earth and cause it to disconnect itself from the power of the Holy Spirit. Once disconnected from God's power and life-giving Spirit, human beings begin to add, substitute, improvise, and synchronize their own philosophy so their conscience can be satisfied. These new philosophies and regulations then begin to work as leaven in an entire group, and can be used to control them with legalism that God never mandated. That is why Jesus said, "Beware." This seems to be the Lord's greatest warning as He walked the earth as an example of the Father's love for us.

GNOSTICISTIC BELIEFS CAN PREVENT THE CHURCH FROM EXPERIENCING POWER

Gnosticism is the modern term for certain religious and philosophical perspectives that existed prior to the establishment of Christianity, and for the specific systems of belief characterized by these ideas which emerged in the second century and later. The term "gnosticism" is derived from the Greek word *gnosis* (knowledge) because secret knowledge was a crucial doctrine in gnosticism. Gnosticism had prominence in history by interjecting much of its thinking into the formation of Christianity. Gnosticism emerged in the church in the early second century and soon established itself as a way of understanding Christianity in all of the church's principal centers.

Gnosticism, or mystery cults, believed that the true God would not enter our world. Therefore, what John and the other true apostles stressed in the Word of God—that Jesus was God's incarnate Son—was dismissed. Once these beliefs crept into the foundation of the Church, the power of a resurrected Christ was negated. When we do not adhere to the power of the full Word of God and declare it inherent, God's power in the earth is diminished. We begin to have a form of religion that denies God's power.

THE CULT OF MITHRAS

In February 2002, I took a team to Rome. We visited the Basilica of St. Clemente. This particular basilica was built upon the ruins of the cult of Mithras which had been recently uncovered. Mithras (who is in reality a demonic spirit seeking worship) was said to be a mediator between the sun god and humanity. Of all the major cults that had influence during the development of the early church, the worship of Mithras was the greatest competitor to Christianity.

This cult practiced secrecy, and its teachings were never recorded. But because the temples were built underground, their contents were preserved remarkably well. Mithraism was powerful and spread more rapidly than Christianity in the Roman Empire. The Roman soldiers of that time took this cult from region to region. It was organized as a series of "grades" or "levels" of initiation through which the Mithraic practitioner gradually rose. These practices are linked very closely with Masonic worship.

Included in every practicing cult, in every possible habitat, was the bull slaying phenomenon, which links the cult to astrological worship. Because of these links to Freemasonry and astrology, we find many of the traces of this worship still being practiced today.

Many have thought that Mithras worship originated in Persia with roots found in modern-day Iran. However, we also find that Tarsus, the city where Paul was raised, seemed to be a center of Mithras worship. Ancient bull worship was also linked with Ashtoreth. As you review the following details, you will see how Stoic, Gnostic beliefs can influence the church and diminish its power on earth.

Why would the Lord lead us to pray concerning this particular form of worship? God has a sure foundation in His church. It is built upon apostles and prophets (see Eph. 2 2:20). This foundation must display God's holy character with no mixture. Ezekiel says that this is a day to separate the holy and profane (see Ez. 22:26). This foundation also has an order. In 1 Corinthians 12:28 we find "first apostles, second prophets..." When this order is in operation and aligned with God's holy character, we see the earth being transformed and God's church functioning the way it should. However, when we find a form of religion that is not in full alignment with God's character and order, we find this religion capturing the minds of people and holding them in bondage.

The team knew this was a key prayer point, and that God had sent us there to repent for the Mithraism that had entered the church and mixed with Christianity. As we prayed, we felt it was time to get the power of Mithras out of the foundation of the church, especially in the Roman Catholic religion. As you read on, you will see how Mithraism has held many in this religion captive.

MITHRAISM AND CATHOLICISM

We declared that all of the bondage that had entered the foundation of the Church where Mithraism and Christianity were syncretized would be exposed. Much of the mindset from this religion has invaded the power of the Lord's life-giving church here in the earth realm. The early church began to embrace many of the methods and administrations that we see in Catholicism today. Not until the Reformation did these practices begin to separate and worship take a different form. We are now in a greater "reformation" for the church's true foundation to be restored. Therefore, it is time for an even deeper separation to occur in false mindsets and practices.

We prayed that there would be an open door now for the veil to be removed from the eyes of many Catholic worshipers so that the true Gospel of the living Lord Jesus Christ could be seen. We prayed for a revival in the life of those in the Catholic Church. It is time for the church to be revived and delivered from the many practices related to the Mithras cult.

Of all the mystery religions, Mithraism became the strongest rival to Christianity. Among the more prominent cultural features are:

1. **December 25 was the god's birthday**. The emperor Aurelian declared December 25 to be the official birthday of Mithras, circa 270 CE. The emperor Constantine was a follower of Mithras until he declared December 25 the official birthday of *Jesus* in 313 CE and adopted Christianity as the state religion.

2. **Sunday the holy day**.

3. **Baptism.**

4. **A sacred meal**. Mithra was said to take a last supper with his followers when he returned to his father.

5. **Belief in a final judgment**. Those who worshiped Mithras believed in eternal life for the righteous and punishment for the wicked. The world would finally be destroyed by fire.

6. **Belief that Mithras did not die, but that he ascended to heaven**. From there he would return at the end of time to

raise the dead in a physical resurrection for a final judgment, sending the good to heaven and the wicked to hell.

7. **He is shown with a nimbus, or halo, around his head.**

8. **Mithras worshipers followed a leader called a 'papa' (pope), who ruled from the Vatican hill in Rome.**

9. **Celebrated *sacramenta*** (a consecrated meal of bread and wine), termed a *Myazda* (corresponding exactly to the Catholic *Missa* (mass), using chanting, bells, candles, incense, and holy water, in remembrance of the last supper of Mithras).

These characteristics are amazing. Look how a cult has influenced our worship. It's time for revival in the church. It's time for the foundation of the church that will influence society in the next 40 years to arise. We must cry for deliverance.

During our time of prayer in the cult of Mithras ruins we drove a "peg" into the ground and prayed the following Scripture from Ezra 9:8-9, "And now for a little while grace has been shown from the LORD our God, to leave us a remnant to escape, and to give us a peg in His holy place, that our God may enlighten our eyes and give us a measure of revival in our bondage. For we were slaves. Yet our God did not forsake us in our bondage; but He extended mercy to us in the sight of the kings of Persia, to revive us, to repair the house of our God."

When we finished praying in Rome, we knew that changes had occurred, and that as a sign, we would see an upheaval begin in the Catholic Church. When we pray, we see an opportunity for change in the earth. This is a time when God is making a sure foundation for the future.

SEEK YE FIRST HIS KINGDOM

Matthew 6:33 says, "But seek first the kingdom of God and His righteousness, and all these things shall be added to you." If we learn to seek God first and are able to prioritize properly in our lives, everything we need will be added to us. In order to do that, our mind is going to have to be renewed, transformed, and learning to think the way that God thinks.

Romans 12:1-2 says, "And so, dear brothers and sisters, I plead with you to give your bodies to God. Let them be a living and holy sacrifice – the kind He will accept. When you think of what He has done for you, is this too much to ask? Don't copy the behaviors and customs of this world, but let God transform you into a new person by changing the way you think. Then you will know what God wants you to do and you will know how good and pleasing and perfect His will really is." Hindering demons attempt to stop our mind from thinking the way God thinks. Demonic forces know that if our minds are operating with God's anointing, we will be able to prioritize and order our steps in the way God intends us to do on a daily basis. We advance and the Kingdom advances. We will be useful tools in God's hands as well as prosperous in our lives.

SUPERSTITION, LEGALISM, AND SPIRITISM

Catholicism is filled with three major issues that hold its subjects captive and keep them from seeking a Holy God. They are superstition, legalism, and spiritism.

SUPERSTITION

Superstition takes a set of rules that must be followed in order to keep evil from our lives. When I was growing up my family had numerous superstitions. If a triggering event occurred, then we had to do 10 other things to neutralize the negative effects that we thought would come as a result of the triggering event. The Bible says superstition is a sign of ignorance. Ignorance has nothing to do with not being educated. Ignorance means that truth has been rejected at some point and the truth is no longer operating.

Superstition binds you to certain behaviors, just as legalism binds you to certain behaviors. Therefore, any time you embrace superstitious beliefs of any nature they produce legalistic thought patterns. The word superstition has its roots in a Greek word indicating fear of or reverence for the gods. The term can be used in a good sense or in a derogatory sense. Modern translations of the Bible usually take the term in the sense of "very religious" or "uncommonly scrupulous" concerning religion.

LEGALISM

Legalism is an attempt to please God by following a religious set of rules. We then bind those rules to ourselves and our thought processes, and make those rules equal to truth rather than allowing the Holy Spirit to be our guide. Have you ever known someone to take a passage from the Word of God and use it as a whipping tool or as binding law? These beliefs, which can seem good, narrow our path and sphere of life in a way God never intended. Legalism works through religious spirits. Many times religious spirits work within the church in superstitious, legalistic forms. They take what God means for liberty and misuse the truth to bring bondage. Paul told the church of Galatia the following:

"Oh, foolish Galatians! What magician has cast an evil spell on you? (Who has bewitched you?) For you used to see the meaning of Jesus Christ's death as clearly as though I had shown you a signboard with a picture of Christ dying on the cross. Let me ask you this one question: Did you receive the Holy Spirit by keeping the law? Of course not, for the Holy Spirit came upon you only after you believed the message you heard about Christ. Have you lost your sense? After starting your Christian lives in the Spirit, why are you now trying to become perfect by our own human effort? You have suffered so much for the Good News. Surely it was not in vain, was it? Are you now going to just throw it all away?" (Galatians 3:1-4, NLT).

SPIRITISM

Spiritism is communicating with familial or familiar spirits linked with the dead. Because Catholics are taught to pray to Mary and the saints, they enter into a form of spiritism. We should never seek help of the dead to advance us into the reality of God's plan.

TRUE WORSHIP IS REALITY

How can one who is entrenched in Catholicism or held in the power of religion enter into spiritual life, freedom and reality?

1. Have no other gods before God. Do not elevate any human above your relationship with Father God, Jesus Christ and the Holy Spirit. Renounce that you have exalted the Pope above Jesus. Break the power and oppression of domination from your mind so that you are no longer motivated by fear.

2. Ask forgiveness for not studying the Bible to show yourself approved (see 2 Timothy 2:15).

3. Ask the Lord for a spirit of revelation to come upon you so the Word of God becomes real to you.

4. Ask the Lord for forgiveness for being involved in rituals and using sacred objects.

5. Ask the Lord to forgive you for using unbiblical prayers which came from mystical experiences of "saints," visions, or apparitions.

6. Ask God to draw you into a real life of prayer.

7. Ask the Lord to forgive you for exalting Mary above Jesus. Thank God for the faith Mary exhibited to bring forth God's plan of redemption. But worship the One and only One who can redeem you.

8. Ask God to break the power of legalism linked with misdirected loyalty, forbidden marriage, forbidden fruits, and doctrines of demons. Let His grace surround and overtake you.

9. Forgive those in the Catholic religion that have not taught you the truth. Bless those who have persecuted you.

10. Ask the Holy Spirit to fill you. He can teach you, train you, comfort you and anoint you for the future.

Communion is worshiping in Spirit and truth. "God is Spirit, and those who worship Him must worship in spirit and truth" (John 4:24). It takes both to produce reality. If you are blocked in the power and strength that you have to worship by a demon force, you cannot gain the daily revelation of who God is. Therefore you never touch Him in worship, and do not know what His will is for your life. Consequently, you don't operate in confidence, but live in insecurity. Worship and communion should be a daily occurrence because it keeps the flow of God's Spirit moving through us. These are days of restoration. Even though you may have been bound in the past by religious forces, the Holy Spirit can restore you to life and you can have life abundantly. Be free! Be filled! Worship Him in Spirit and in truth.

GLOSSARY
OF SOME CATHOLIC TERMS

ABBESS. The superior of a community of nuns.

ABBEY. A large, independent monastery which is governed by an abbott or an abbess.

ABBOT. The superior of a community of monks.

ABSOLUTION. According to Catholic doctrine, in the sacrament of penance (confession), after the penitent confesses his or her sins and says a prayer of repentance, a qualified priest can absolve the penitent from his or her sins by saying a verbal formula. The words of absolution presently used were instituted by the Second Vatican Council (1962-1965). (See "Penitent")

ADORATION OF THE BLESSED SACRAMENT (Eucharist). According to Catholic doctrine, Jesus Christ is literally present in consecrated bread and wine. The Council of Trent declared that the body, blood, soul and divinity of Jesus Christ are literally present. Therefore the custom of venerating the Blessed Sacrament is encouraged. A consecrated Host (a large Communion wafer with a decorative pattern on it) is placed in a monstrance (a container which can stand on the altar, contains the Host, and has a glass front which enables people to see the Host). People worship the Host as if it was Jesus Christ Himself, in person, in front of them. If this is done in a special service, it ends with Benediction. A priest holds up the monstrance and makes the sign of the cross over the people with it, and pronounces a blessing. (See "Eucharist" and "Monstrance")

ADVENT. The four weeks before Christmas.

ADVENT WREATH. Four candles (tapirs) surrounded by a wreath of green foliage. On the first Sunday of Advent, one candle is lit. The second Sunday, two candles are lit. The third Sunday, three candles are lit. The fourth Sunday, all four candles are lit. In some countries, the lighting of the candles is accompanied by special ceremonies which include songs and prayers.

ALTAR. The table on which the Sacrifice of the Mass is offered. It usually contains one or more relics of martyrs. (See "Relics" and "Altar Stone")

ALTAR STONE. A small, flat stone which is consecrated by a bishop. It has a cavity which contains the relics of two canonized martyrs. It is usually inserted in the center of an altar. During Mass, the Host and chalice are placed on top of the altar stone.

ANATHEMA. A solemn ecclesiastical curse which is accompanied by excommunication. There is a formal, written ritual for doing it.

ANOINTING OF THE SICK. (See "Sacrament") A sacrament in which the priest anoints the hands and forehead of the sick person, using olive oil which has been blessed by a bishop. He says a prayer which is a standard verbal formula. This is also called the Last Rites, or Extreme Unction.

APOSTOLIC SEE (Holy See). The official residence of the Pope in Rome. The offices of Vatican officials are located there. The term also refers to the power and authority of the Pope.

APPARITION. A supernatural being which manifests itself to an individual or individuals. The most frequent apparition is the Virgin Mary. When she appears, often only one person can see and hear her, but other people who are present cannot. At some apparition sites, many people see her, but most of the crowd cannot. Apparitions may be accompanied by supernatural signs and wonders such as rose petals falling out of the sky, people being healed, or the "miracle of the sun." The "miracle of the sun" first occurred at Fatima in 1917, where it was seen by about 120 people. The sun appeared to plummet towards the earth. It looked like it was going to crash onto the people and they were terrified. Then suddenly the sun went back to its proper place in the sky. Since then, the "miracle of the sun" has accompanied some other apparitions of Mary. Lourdes, Fatima and some other apparitions of Mary have been officially approved by the Catholic Church. However, many Christians believe that these apparitions are actually manifestations of demons who are disguising themselves as Mary. Jesus warned us that the End Times would be accompanied by great deception. (See Matthew 24:4, 11, 24.) The Apostle Paul said that there is such a thing as "lying signs and wonders" whose purpose is to deceive people. (See 2 Thessalonians 2:9.) He also said that Satan can disguise himself as an angel of light. (See 2 Corinthians 11:14.) The apparitions of Mary are accompanied by light. One apparition (in Zeitoun, Egypt) was a woman made out of light. This apparition was unusual because everybody could see it and it could be photographed. It appeared above a church every day for three years. There would be flashes of light, followed by something which looked like an explosion of stars, followed by a brilliant light. Then a woman made of light appeared above the church, moving like a real person.

ASH WEDNESDAY. The first day of Lent. Priests put ashes on the foreheads of the people. These are special ashes which are made by burning the palms from the previous year's Palm Sunday.

ASSUMPTION OF MARY. The doctrine that at the end of her life, Mary was taken up ("assumed") body and soul into Heaven.

ATONE. To make amends for an offense; to expiate; to restore harmony between individuals. (See "Expiate")

ATONEMENT. When Jesus Christ voluntarily died on the cross, He satisfied the legitimate demands of God the Father. He made amends for the sinful wrongdoing of mankind. He repaired the breach caused by these offenses. This is called making reparation for sin. According to the Catholic Church, when God forgives sins He may still require that the sinner atone for his or her sins by suffering either here on earth or else in Purgatory. This is called "temporal punishment." (See "Purgatory")

AURICULAR CONFESSION. (See "Sacrament") According to Catholic doctrine, people who commit mortal sins after they are baptized are required to confess their sins to a qualified priest in order to receive absolution from their sins. The term "auricular" is used because normally the sins are confessed out loud and heard by the ears of the priest. This sacrament is also known as Confession, the Sacrament of Penance, and the Sacrament of Reconciliation. (See "Mortal Sin")

BAPTISM. (See "Sacrament") According to Catholic doctrine, the sacrament of baptism cleanses the person who is baptized from all sin (both original sin and sins which the person committed before being baptized). As a result, he or she becomes reborn and sanctified in Christ. It is the sacrament that is said to remove the sin, rather than the repentance of the person baptized. It is the sacrament that is said to cause spiritual rebirth, rather than the faith of the person baptized or their relationship with God.

BAPTISMAL GRACES. These are the supernatural results of the sacrament of baptism. According to Catholic doctrine, baptism removes all of the guilt of sin (both original sin and sins which the person committed before being baptized). It removes all of the punishment due for sins committed before baptism. It removes both temporal punishment (on earth or in Purgatory) and eternal punishment (in hell). It infuses sanctifying grace into the person. It infuses faith, hope and charity into the person. It makes the person a member of the Mystical Body of Christ.

BAPTISMAL WATER. (See "Sacramentals"). A special kind of holy water which is used for administering the sacrament of baptism. Baptismal water is ritually blessed on Holy Saturday.

BEATIFICATION. A declaration by the Pope that a deceased man or woman lived a holy life or died a martyr's death and is now in Heaven. People who have been beatified are given the title "Blessed." Catholics are allowed to venerate them. Canonization requires that Catholics venerate the saint. Beatification (the step before canonization) allows veneration but does not require it.

BENEDICTION. A priest holds up a monstrance which contains a consecrated Host. He makes the sign of the cross over the people with it, and pronounces a blessing. (See "Host" and "Monstrance")

BIRETTA. A square cap with three ridges or peaks on its upper surface. Cardinals wear scarlet. Bishops wear purple. Priests wear black.

BISHOP. According to Catholic doctrine, a bishop is a successor of the Apostles and he has received the fullness of the priesthood of Christ. Bishops have the power to ordain priests.

BLESSED. (1) A sacramental (a blessed object). (2) A deceased man or woman who has been beatified by the Catholic Church. (3) A person, place or thing which is associated with God.

BLESSED SACRAMENT (the Eucharist). Bread and wine which have been consecrated by a priest. (The priest has performed the ritual of consecration using the correct verbal formula.) According to Catholic doctrine, they literally become the body, blood, soul and divinity of Jesus Christ. The Catholic Church uses Communion wafers instead of regular bread.

BLESSED SALT. (See "Sacramentals") Salt which has been blessed by a priest. There is a ritual with an official prayer to be used for this blessing. Blessed salt is a sacramental which people use to protect themselves from the corruption of evil, such as sickness, demonic influence, and temptations which seem to be overwhelming. Some common uses for blessed salt are sprinkling it across thresholds or in cars for protection, or putting it in food or drinking water for physical healing.

BREVIARY. A liturgical book which contains the Divine Office. (See "Divine Office")

BROWN SCAPULAR. (See "Scapular") On July 16, 1251, the Virgin Mary appeared to St. Simon Stock, the Father General of the Carmelite Order. Mary was carrying the brown scapular. She promised that people who are wearing the brown scapular when they die will not go to hell. She said that this scapular is a sign of salvation and protection. Wearing the brown scapular also enables people to receive the benefits of the Sabbatine Privilege. The use of the brown scapular has been strongly recommended by many popes, including Pope Paul VI

(1963-1978). (See "Sabbatine Privilege")

BULL (Papal Bull). A papal letter which carries a special seal (a *bulla*) because of the importance of its subject matter.

CANDLE. (See "Sacramentals") When used in the liturgy of the Catholic Church, candles are sacramentals. Candles can also be used in private devotional practices. Examples are votive candles placed in front of statues of Jesus, Mary, and the saints. Some people use novena candles in association with novena prayers. (See "Votive Candles" and "Novena Candles")

CANDLEMAS. The feast of the Purification of Mary (February 2). Candles are blessed on that day. Processions with lighted candles are held.

CANON OF THE MASS. The Eucharistic Prayer (words of consecration). This is the most important part of the Sacrifice of the Mass. (See "Consecration")

CANON LAW. An official compilation of the laws governing the Catholic Church.

CANONIZATION. An official declaration by the Pope that a deceased man or woman is a saint. Canonization requires that Catholics venerate the saint. Beatification (the step before canonization) allows veneration but does not require it.

CANONIZED. A saint who has been through the process of canonization.

CARDINAL. Next to the papacy, this is the highest office in the Catholic Church. The cardinals are members of the Sacred College, which assists the Pope with the government of the Catholic Church. Originally men became popes by various means. Then the practice developed of having the cardinals elect the popes. In modern times, popes are required to be cardinals in order to qualify for the papacy. Cardinals are allowed to wear a scarlet biretta (a special hat) and a scarlet cassock (a long clerical garment) and a scarlet zucchetto (skullcap). (See "Biretta," "Cassock," and "Zucchetto")

CASSOCK. A long clerical garment which reaches to the feet. Cardinals are allowed to wear scarlet cassocks.

CATHEDRAL. The official church of a bishop.

CHALICE. A large goblet used at Mass to contain the wine for consecration. If the chalice is not made of gold, then the inside must be gold-plated. A chalice is consecrated by a bishop, using holy chrism. (See "Chrism")

CHAPLET. Chaplets are prayers said using beads. Some of them, such as the Chaplet of Divine Mercy, use regular rosary beads but with different prayers. Others, such as the Chaplet of St. Michael the Arch-angel and the Chaplet of St. Joseph, use different beads. For example, the Chaplet of St. Michael has nine sets of one large bead followed by three small beads.

CHRISM. A mixture of olive oil and balsam (an aromatic, oily, resin-ous substance). Chrism is consecrated by being blessed by a bishop. It is used in the sacraments of baptism, confirmation, and holy orders (ordination). It is used when blessing baptismal water and church tower bells. It is used in consecrating churches, altars, chalices, and patens. (See "Consecrate" and "Paten")

CIBORIUM. A covered container which holds small consecrated Hosts for Communion. It is similar to a chalice, but larger. It is covered, and used to give Communion to the people who attend Mass. The inside of the ciborium is gold or gold-plated.

CLERGY. Men who are ordained as deacons, priests or bishops.

CLERIC. A clergyman.

CLOISTER. A monastery or convent. In a strictly cloistered convent, the nuns are cut off from the rest of the world. When visitors (includ-ing family members) come to see them, they must sit with a grille between them. They can talk with the nun but they cannot make any kind of physical contact.

COMMUNION (Holy Communion, the Eucharist). (See "Sacrament") Bread and wine which have been consecrated by a priest. (The priest has performed the ritual of consecration using the correct verbal for-mula.) According to Catholic doctrine, the bread and wine literally become the body, blood, soul and divinity of Jesus Christ. The term "taking Communion" means eating the consecrated bread. The Catholic Church uses Communion wafers instead of regular bread. Catholics sometimes drink the consecrated wine from the chalice, but usually they just eat the Communion wafers without drinking the wine. Some-times the Communion wafers are dipped into consecrated wine.

COMMUNION OF SAINTS. The doctrine that there is unity among the members of the Catholic Church on earth, in Heaven, and in Pur-gatory, and that they help one another through prayers and good works. Catholics on earth are said to be in communion with the saints in Heaven by venerating them, imitating them, and invoking their prayers and assistance. They are said to be in communion with the souls in Purgatory by helping them with prayers and good works. This in-cludes things such as having Masses said for them, earning indul-gences on their behalf, or offering up their own sufferings to atone for the sins of their deceased loved ones. (See "Mystical Body of Christ")

COMMUNION WAFERS. These are round and flat. There is a large Communion wafer called the Host, which is used by the priest. It has a decorative design on it. Small Communion wafers are eaten by the people who attend Mass.

CONCLAVE. During an election for a new Pope, the cardinals are kept enclosed in the Sistine Chapel (the Pope's private chapel). (See "Sistine Chapel")

CONCORDAT. A treaty made between the Pope and the ruler (or rulers) of a sovereign nation.

CONFESSION. (See "Sacrament") According to Catholic doctrine, people who commit mortal sins after they are baptized are required to confess their sins to a qualified priest in order to receive absolution from their sins. This sacrament is also known as the Sacrament of Penance, and the Sacrament of Reconciliation.

CONFESSIONAL. The enclosed place where a priest sits to hear confessions. There is also an enclosed place where the penitent sits to confess his or her sins, separated from the priest by a partition which has a screened window in it.

CONFESSOR. A priest who hears confessions and absolves sins.

CONFIRMATION. (See "Sacrament") A sacrament which is said to cause baptized Catholics to be strengthened by the Holy Spirit. It involves the laying on of hands and anointing with chrism.

CONSECRATE. To declare something to be holy or to make it holy. To set something apart for service to God or worship of God.

CONSECRATION. An event which occurs during Mass. The priest says a precise verbal formula. At that point, according to Catholic doctrine, the bread and wine literally become the body, blood, soul and divinity of Jesus Christ. This is called the consecration of the bread and wine. The consecrated bread and wine are referred to as the Eucharist or the Blessed Sacrament. The Catholic Church uses Communion wafers instead of regular bread.

CONTEMPLATIVE LIFE. Religious life which stresses prayer and self-denial.

CONVENT (Nunnery). A community of nuns.

CRUCIFIX. A cross which bears an image of Christ being crucified.

CRUSADES. Military expeditions which were instigated by popes or done with their sanction. The first crusades were attempts to recover the Holy Land from the Muslims. One crusade conquered and pillaged Constantinople (the Orthodox Church's equivalent of Rome). The Massacre of the Albigensians was called a crusade.

CULT. A group of people who are devoted to particular religious observances. They are often focussed on worship of saints or apparitions of Mary.

CURIA (Roman Curia). Administrative and judicial offices which are located in the Vatican. They assist the Pope in directing the operations of the Catholic Church.

CZESTOCHOWA (the Black Madonna). Miracles have been attributed to a painting of Mary which is in Czestochowa, Poland. Five million pilgrims come every year to venerate it. In addition, there are many chapels around the world which have replicas of the painting.

DECADE. There are five sets of decades in a rosary. Each decade consists of one large bead and ten small beads. The "Our Father" (Lord's Prayer) is said on the large beads. The "Hail Mary" is said on the small beads. The words of the "Hail Mary" are, "Hail Mary full of grace, the Lord is with thee. Blessed art thou among women and blessed is the fruit of thy womb, Jesus. Holy Mary, mother of God, pray for us sinners, now and at the hour of our death."

DIVINE OFFICE. An official book with psalms, hymns, prayers, antiphons, and Scripture passages. It is read by priests, monks and nuns. It is organized according to the seasons of the Catholic Church (Advent, Lent, etc.), feast days of saints, and holy days. The Divine Office may be read privately or publicly. In some religious communities, the psalms, hymns and antiphons are sung publicly.

ECSTASY. An altered state of consciousness resulting from a mystical experience. It has physical, mental and spiritual manifestations. When saints and seers were in an ecstasy, sometimes people would test their condition by doing painful things, such as sticking needles into them. It was considered to be a sign of a true ecstasy if the saint or seer was unaware of what was physically happening to them.

ENCYCLICAL. A document which the Pope sends to the bishops dealing with matters related to the general welfare of the Catholic Church. Encyclicals often contain pronouncements about matters of faith and morals.

EPIPHANY. A feast day which commemorates the magi (wise men) coming to see the infant Jesus in Bethlehem. It also commemorates the baptism of Jesus and the miracle at the wedding in Cana. It occurs on the twelfth day after Christmas. In some countries it is a holy day of obligation. (See "Holy Days of Obligation")

EUCHARIST (the Blessed Sacrament). (See "Sacrament") Bread and wine which have been consecrated by a priest. (The priest has performed the ritual of consecration using the correct verbal formula.) According to Catholic doctrine, the bread and wine literally become the body, blood, soul and divinity of Jesus Christ. The Catholic Church uses Communion wafers instead of regular bread.

EX CATHEDRA. A declaration made by the Pope when he speaks with the weight of his apostolic authority, as opposed to speaking as a private theologian.

EXCOMMUNICATION. Expelling an individual, or a group of people, from the Catholic Church. The most severe form of excommunication is the anathema, which can be inflicted with formal solemnities (a formal ritual in which the anathematized person is cursed and cut off from the Catholic Church). Excommunication can be automatically incurred as a result of committing particular offenses. For example, heretics are automatically excommunicated. It can also be inflicted as a penalty by the Pope or his representatives.

EXPIATE. To make complete satisfaction for offenses; to appease; to atone.

EXPIATION. To atone for wrongdoing; to appease the person who has been offended by the wrongdoing; propitiation.

EXTREME UNCTION. (See "Sacrament") A sacrament in which a priest anoints the hands and forehead of the sick person, using olive oil which has been blessed by a bishop. He says a prayer which is a standard verbal formula. This is also called the Anointing of the Sick, or the Last Rites.

FASTING. A form of penance which involves abstaining from particular foods or limiting the quantity of foods eaten. Fasting requirements are determined by the Catholic Church hierarchy and the rules change from time to time. The custom of eating fish on Fridays developed because for a long time Catholics were not allowed to eat the meat of birds or land animals on Fridays, but eating fish was allowed. During Lent, there are requirements for both fasting and abstinence. At present, this means abstaining from the meat of birds or land animals on Ash Wednesday and all Fridays during Lent. It also means limiting the amount of food eaten on those days. Catholics can eat one full meal. The amount of food allowed during the rest of the day is determined by the bishops. During the Middle Ages, fasting requirements were more severe. Catholics were not allowed to drink wine or to eat meat during the entire 40 days of Lent. In some countries, they were not allowed to eat any animal products at all, including butter, milk, eggs, and cheese. (See "Lent")

FATIMA. The Virgin Mary appeared to three children (Lucia, Jacinta, and Francisco) in Fatima, Portugal. She appeared once a month from May 13 to October 13, 1917. She told them many things about the state of the world and what would happen in the future. She said that people should pray the rosary and consecrate themselves to her Immaculate Heart. She also said that the Pope should consecrate the entire world to her Immaculate Heart. (Pope John Paul II has done it.) Over four million pilgrims come to Fatima every year.

FINAL PENITENCE. Having one's sins be absolved before dying.

FINAL PERSEVERANCE. Remaining steadfast in goodness until death. Being in a state of grace at the moment of death. (See "State of Grace")

FINGER ROSARY. A rosary with only one decade (in a circle) and a crucifix. It is small, with the beads touching each other. It is often made of metal and it looks like a ring. People can put it on their finger like a ring and count the beads with their thumb. Each time they say a "Hail Mary" they can use their thumb to move the ring to the next position. When they reach the cross, they know that they have completed the decade. (See "Decade")

FIRST FRIDAYS. In 1699, St. Margaret Mary Alacoque had an apparition of Jesus. He asked her to observe the "Devotion of First Fridays" (receiving Communion on the first Friday of nine consecutive months). He also asked that people keep a picture of the Sacred Heart of Jesus in their homes and honor it. He gave 12 promises to people who venerate His Sacred Heart. One of them is a promise that their names will be written in Jesus' Heart and will never be blotted out. The apparition of Jesus promised that people who observe the "Devotion of First Fridays" will have the grace of final penitence; they will not die without receiving the sacraments; and the Sacred Heart of Jesus will be their safe refuge at the moment of death.

FIRST SATURDAYS. Our Lady of Fatima gave promises of things she would do for people who observe the "Devotion of First Saturdays." In order to fulfill the conditions for receiving the promises, they have to do several things on the first Saturday of five consecutive months. These include going to confession, receiving Communion, praying the rosary, spending 15 minutes "keeping Mary company" while meditating on the 15 mysteries of the rosary, and consecrating themselves to the Immaculate Heart of Mary. The 15 mysteries of the rosary are five joyful mysteries (such as the Annunciation), five sorrowful mysteries (such as the Crucifixion), and five glorious mysteries (such as the Ascension). These acts are to be performed with the intention of making reparation to Mary for sin.

FLAGELLANTS. People who whip or scourge themselves or one another as an act of penance or atonement for sin. On Good Friday, some countries have processions of flagellants who whip themselves as they walk through the streets.

FLAGELLATE. To flog, whip, scourge. Some religious congregations have used flagellation as a form of penance, to mortify the body and to atone for sin. Some saints were know for whipping themselves.

GENUFLECT. To bend the knee as an act of reverence or worship. One knee goes down to the floor and the other knee remains bent. It is traditional to genuflect before the Blessed Sacrament and before entering a church pew for worship. It is also traditional to genuflect before the Pope, a cardinal, and one's own bishop. This is often accompanied by kissing their ring.

GOOD FRIDAY. The Friday before Easter. This day commemorates the crucifixion of Jesus.

GREEN SCAPULAR (the Cloth of Conversion). (See "Scapular") In 1840 the Virgin Mary appeared to Sister Justine Bisqueyburu carrying the green scapular. On the front it had a picture of the Immaculate Heart of Mary. On the back it had a picture of Mary's heart, pierced with a sword, with drops of blood coming out of it. In a circle around the heart was written a prayer, "Immaculate Heart of Mary, pray for us now and at the hour of our death." Cures and conversions are attributed to the green scapular.

HABIT. The distinctive clothing worn by monks and nuns.

HAIL MARY (Ave Maria). The words of this prayer are, "Hail Mary full of grace, the Lord is with thee. Blessed art thou among women and blessed is the fruit of thy womb, Jesus. Holy Mary, mother of God, pray for us sinners, now and at the hour of our death."

HAIR SHIRT. A shirt made of horsehair which is worn as a penance. (It makes people itch.)

HERESY. According to the Catholic Church, any belief which is opposed to Catholic doctrine, and which claims to be Christian, is heresy.

HERETIC. According to the Catholic Church, in order to be considered heretics, people must have been baptized. (This is not limited to baptism in the Catholic Church. It includes any Christian baptism.) They must claim to be Christians. They must deny a Catholic doctrine or have a "positive doubt" about it. And their disbelief must be "morally culpable." Protestants satisfy the first three requirements. The Catholic Church would decide whether or not it considers their disbelief to be "morally culpable." During the Protestant Reformation, men and women who had been born and raised as Protestants were condemned as heretics and killed on orders of the Inquisition.

HOLY CARDS. These are cards which have religious pictures related to Catholicism such as Jesus, Mary, the Holy Family, saints, Michael the Archangel, popes, or shrines. There usually is a prayer on the back of the card, or a note commemorating a special event such as a child's first Communion.

HOLY CHRISM. A mixture of olive oil and balsam (an aromatic, oily, resinous substance). Chrism is consecrated by being blessed by a bishop. It is used in the sacraments of baptism, confirmation, and holy orders (ordination). It is used when blessing baptismal water and church tower bells. It is used in consecrating churches, altars, chalices, and patens. (See "Consecrate" and "Paten")

HOLY COMMUNION (the Eucharist). (See "Sacrament") Bread and wine which have been consecrated by a priest. (The priest has performed the ritual of consecration using the correct verbal formula.) According to Catholic doctrine, the bread and wine literally become the body, blood, soul and divinity of Jesus Christ. The term "taking Communion" means eating the consecrated bread. The Catholic Church uses Communion wafers instead of regular bread. Catholics sometimes drink the consecrated wine from the chalice, but usually they just eat the Communion wafers without drinking the wine. Sometimes the Communion wafers are dipped into consecrated wine.

HOLY DAYS OF OBLIGATION. Special days on which Catholics are required to attend Mass. Attendance at Mass is mandatory for Catholics on Sundays and on holy days of obligation. In some places, Mass attendance on Saturday afternoon fulfills the Sunday obligation.

HOLY FATHER. (1) A term which Jesus Christ used to address God the Father (John 17:11). (2) A term which Catholics use when addressing the Pope.

HOLY LAND. The physical location of the places where Jesus Christ lived, ministered, died, and was resurrected (Israel).

HOLY OFFICE. Another name for the Office of the Inquisition. It is located in the Vatican. In 1965 its name was changed to "The Congregation for the Doctrine of the Faith." It is presently headed by Cardinal Ratzinger.

HOLY OILS. (See "Sacramentals") Holy oils for liturgical use are blessed by a bishop. There are three kinds of holy oil: oil of catechumens (used for baptism), chrism, and oil of the sick (for anointing the sick). Oil of catechumens and oil of the sick are pure olive oil. Chrism is a mixture of olive oil with balm or balsam (an aromatic, oily, resinous substance). Holy oils are used for the sacraments of baptism, confirmation, and the anointing of the sick. The blessing of the holy oils is usually done on Holy Thursday by a bishop, in a cathedral. The oils are distributed to local churches where they are kept in locked boxes. Any oil which is not used within a year is burned in the sanctuary lamp. Holy oils for use in homes are usually taken from oil lamps burning at shrines. Some examples are Saint Anne's Oil, Saint Joseph's Oil, and Saint Philomena's Oil.

HOLY ORDERS. (See "Sacrament") The sacrament of holy orders. Ordination of a deacon, priest or bishop.

HOLY SATURDAY. The Saturday before Easter.

HOLY SEE (Apostolic See). The official residence of the Pope in Rome. The offices of Vatican officials are located there. The term also refers to the power and authority of the Pope.

HOLY WATER. (See "Sacramentals") Holy water is blessed by a priest who invokes God's blessing on every person who uses it. When Catholics enter a Catholic Church they often dip their fingers in holy water and make the sign of the cross. All official blessings by the Catholic Church include the use of holy water. In addition to ordinary holy water there are also some special kinds of holy water. Baptismal holy water is used in the sacrament of baptism. Easter holy water is used during the Paschal Season. Chrism is used in the blessing of holy water. Many Catholics keep holy water in their homes and use it during times of physical or spiritual danger. People can sprinkle it around the house, sprinkle it on family members, and even drink it. (See "Paschal Season" and "Chrism")

HOLY WEEK. The week before Easter.

HOST. A large, round wafer used by the priest when saying Mass.

IMMACULATE CONCEPTION. The doctrine that Mary was conceived without any stain of original sin.

IMMACULATE HEART OF MARY. There is a picture which represents the Immaculate Heart of Mary. It shows Mary with her chest open, her heart exposed, flames above it, light coming out of it, and a sword piercing it. This is an object of devotion for many Catholics. Our Lady of Fatima gave a prayer for people to use when consecrating themselves to the Immaculate Heart of Mary.

IMMACULATE HEART PROMISES (the Great Promise). In 1925, Our Lady of Fatima appeared to Blessed Lucia and promised that if any person fulfills the conditions of the "Devotion of First Saturdays," then Mary will help them when they die by providing the grace needed for their salvation.

INCENSE. (See "Sacramentals") An aromatic gum or resin which is in the form of powder or grains so that it can readily be burned. It

gives off a fragrant smoke. Incense which has been blessed is a sacramental. It is used during Mass, at Benediction of the Blessed Sacrament, during processions, and at absolutions of the dead. Five large
grains of incense are placed in the Paschal Candle, symbolizing the
five wounds of Christ.

INDULGENCES. According to Catholic doctrine, when God forgives
sins He may still require that the sinner atone for those sins by suffering (either here on earth or else in Purgatory). In other words, although Jesus Christ died to pay for our sins, God the Father may also
require us to pay for them by suffering. This is called "temporal punishment." According to the Catholic Church, there is a "treasury" of
merits which have been won by Christ and the saints. It is said that the
Catholic Church is able to draw from this "treasury" in order to remit
the temporal punishments which are required for sins which have already been forgiven by God. This is done by means of indulgences.
The Catholic Church grants indulgences for certain good works. In
modern times, earning indulgences is done primarily by means of indulgenced prayers and religious devotions (such as praying the rosary)
for which the Catholic Church has granted indulgences. During the
Middle Ages, indulgences were sold for money. Indulgences can be
applied to the person earning them or to loved ones who are in Purgatory.

INFALLIBILITY. The doctrine that God protects the Pope from making errors whenever he teaches the Catholic Church in matters of faith
or morals. In order to speak infallibly, the Pope must speak *ex cathedra*. This means that he is declaring that something is unchangeably
true, and he is speaking with the weight of his apostolic authority, as
opposed to speaking as a private theologian. However, according to
Canon Law, Catholics are required to submit their minds and wills to
any declaration concerning faith or morals which is made by the Pope.
They are also required to avoid anything that disagrees with such dec-
larations, and they can be coerced if they don't comply (*Code of Canon
Law*, Canons 752, 1311, 1312). In other words, they must respond as
if the statement is infallible, whether or not the Pope has spoken *ex
cathedra*. This gives the Catholic Church the power derived from
claims of infallibility, without requiring the accountability which would
be associated with infallibility. If one infallible papal pronouncement
contradicts another infallible papal pronouncement, then the theologians and apologists can avoid the dilemma by saying that one (or
both) of the popes was just speaking as a private theologian. (See
"Canon Law")

INFANT OF PRAGUE. A statue of the Infant Jesus is kept in a convent in Prague, Czechoslovakia. Miracles have been attributed to this statue. Pilgrims come from around the world to venerate it. The statue has a gold crown and over 70 sets of ornate clothes. Nuns dress it and change its clothes. Replicas of the statue are found in Catholic churches around the world.

INQUISITION. The Office of the Inquisition is a special court which was appointed by the Pope to systematically suppress heresy and to seek out "heretics" and punish them. It appointed Inquisitors and sent them out to find "heretics." The Inquisitors tortured "heretics" to get confessions, they had trials in which the Inquisitors were the judges while the "heretics" had no one to defend them, and they passed sentences on the "heretics." The Inquisitors required the local civil authorities to execute the sentences. The Office of the Inquisition still exists but its name has been changed. (See "Holy Office")

INTERDICT. Catholics under interdict are not allowed to have a Christian burial or receive some of the sacraments. However, dying people are allowed to receive the Last Rites. The interdict is imposed as a vindictive penalty because of something which has been done which is considered to be contrary to the common good of the Catholic Church.

LAST RITES. (See "Sacrament") A sacrament in which a priest anoints the hands and forehead of the sick person, using olive oil which has been blessed by a bishop. He says a prayer which is a standard verbal formula. This is also called the Anointing of the Sick, or Extreme Unction.

LENT. A 40 day period of prayer and penance before Easter. It begins on Ash Wednesday and ends on Easter Sunday. During Lent, Catholics are required to observe the days of penitence (Ash Wednesday and all Fridays). This includes both fasting and abstinence. Fasting requirements are determined by the Catholic Church hierarchy and the rules change from time to time. The custom of eating fish on Fridays developed because for a long time Catholics were not allowed to eat the meat of birds or land animals on Fridays, but eating fish was allowed. At present, the Lenten fasting rules require Catholics to abstain from eating the meat of birds or land animals on Ash Wednesday and on all Fridays during Lent. The fasting rules also limit the amount of food eaten on those days. Catholics can eat one full meal. The amount of food allowed during the rest of the day is determined by the bishops.

LIMBO. According to the Catholic Church, if a baby is not baptized, then the baby cannot go to Heaven because he or she has the stain of original sin. However, because the baby has not actually committed any sins, he or she does not go to hell. Therefore, unbaptized babies go to Limbo. This is a place of happiness but people there do not have the joy of seeing God face to face.

LITANY.   A structured form of prayer which includes petitions and responses. Litanies to Mary include addressing her by a series of titles. Some of these titles are: Queen of Heaven, Star of the Sea, Mystical Rose, Conceived without Sin, Tower of David, Ark of the Covenant, Mother of God, Mother of our Creator, Mother of the Church, Mirror of Justice, Gate of Heaven, Morning Star, Health of the Sick, Refuge of Sinners, Queen of Angels, Queen of all Saints, Queen of the Most Holy Rosary, Queen of Peace, and Comforter of the Afflicted. The Catholic Church gives indulgences for reciting some of the litanies.

LITURGICAL BOOKS.   Books which have been approved by the Holy See for liturgical use. They contain prayers, hymns and readings.

LITURGY.   Official public worship of the Catholic Church, as opposed to private devotions.

LOCUTION.   Hearing voices from supernatural sources. They can be audibly heard in the ear or heard in the mind.

LOURDES.   In 1858, the Virgin Mary appeared several times to Saint Bernadette Soubirous in Lourdes, France. On one occasion a spring miraculously appeared. People went into this river. Some of them were healed. Pilgrims who visit Lourdes often bring bottles of the water home with them. Bottles of Lourdes water can be purchased in some religious stores and through the Internet. Six million pilgrims come to Lourdes every year.

MASS.   (See "Sacrament") A propitiatory sacrifice in which Christ is sacrificed on the altar in order to appease God the Father. The most important part of the Mass is the consecration of the bread and wine. According to Catholic doctrine, consecrated bread and wine literally become the body, blood, soul and divinity of Jesus Christ. The Catholic Church uses Communion wafers instead of regular bread.

MASS CARDS.   When a Catholic dies, it is traditional for Catholic friends and relatives to give Mass Cards to the family. These cards show that provision has been made for Masses to be said on behalf of the soul of the deceased person. It is traditional to give money to the priests who say the Masses for the deceased. The purpose of the Masses is to help the soul of the deceased person get out of Purgatory. (See "Communion of Saints," "Temporal Punishment," and "Purgatory")

MATRIMONY.   (See "Sacrament") The sacrament of marriage.

MAUNDY THURSDAY. Thursday in Holy Week (the week before Easter).

MEATLESS DAYS. Days on which Catholics are required to abstain from eating the flesh of birds or land animals.

MEDAL. (See "Sacramentals") Metal disks which are usually round. They have a religious image on them such as Jesus, Mary, saints, popes, shrines, or commemorations of sacred events. Sometimes they have prayers on them. The Catholic Church grants indulgences for wearing certain medals.

MIRACULOUS MEDAL (Medal of the Immaculate Conception). On November 27, 1830, the Virgin Mary appeared to St. Catherine Laboure. Mary carried a medal with a picture of herself on it. The medal had an inscription which said "O Mary, conceived without sin, pray for us who have recourse to thee." Mary showed St. Catherine the front and the back of the medal and instructed her to have medals made according to the design shown to her. The medals were made and many people who wore them were reported to have experienced miracles. Because of this, the medal became known as the Miraculous Medal.

MITER. A liturgical headdress which is worn by popes, cardinals, abbots and bishops.

MONASTERY. A secluded place where monks live in community. It applies primarily to religious who live a contemplative life and recite or sing the Divine Office together. Convents of contemplative nuns are sometimes referred to as monasteries. (See "Divine Office")

MONASTICISM. A way of life characterized by asceticism, self-denial, and seclusion from the world.

MONK. Originally the term meant a hermit. It presently means a member of a religious community of men. The most strict use of the term means men who have taken solemn perpetual vows (vows until death). The broad sense of the term includes new monks (novices) and monks who have made temporary vows.

MONSTRANCE. A sacred vessel which contains a consecrated Host. It is used during Adoration of the Blessed Sacrament, Benediction, and in processions. In appearance it looks like a sunburst on top of a pedestal. The monstrance is gold or gold-plated. A large, round consecrated Host goes into a round compartment in the center of the sunburst. It is covered by a glass door. This protects the Host while at the same time enabling people to see it. (See "Benediction")

MORTAL SIN. Sin which is so serious that it destroys the supernatural life of the soul, resulting in spiritual death. When a person is baptized, his or her soul receives spiritual life. If the person commits a mortal sin, then the result is spiritual death. (That is why it is called a "mortal" sin. It kills the soul.) Confession (the Sacrament of Penance) restores spiritual life to the soul when the sin is absolved by a priest. Another mortal sin would cause spiritual death, which would be followed by spiritual life if the sin is absolved. Some examples of things which can be mortal sins are: murder, rape, adultery, missing Mass on Sunday or a holy day of obligation, and eating meat on a meatless day. In order to be absolved of a mortal sin, a Catholic must go to confession (the Sacrament of Penance). (See "Holy Days of Obligation" and "Meatless Days")

MYSTICAL BODY OF CHRIST. All of the members of the Catholic Church, including Mary, the saints, and deceased Catholics. It consists of the Church militant (the Church on the earth), the Church suffering (the souls in Purgatory), and the Church triumphant (the saints in Heaven). (See "Communion of Saints")

NOVENA. Nine consecutive days of prayer for a special request from Jesus, Mary or a saint. It can be nine days in a row, the same day of the week for nine consecutive weeks, the first Friday or first Saturday of nine consecutive months, etc. There are many standard novena prayers. They can be prayed publicly or privately.

NOVENA CANDLES. Large candles in glass holders. They are associated with novena prayers. Although a novena takes nine days, some novena candles only burn for five days or seven days. But there are novena candles which do burn for nine days. Novena candles often have a picture of Jesus, Mary or a saint on one side of the glass container, and a written prayer on the other side of it. Novena candles used to be readily available in Catholic stores. They are not as widely used as they used to be and therefore they have become more difficult to obtain. They can sometimes be found in Hispanic stores, including the Hispanic section of some supermarkets.

NOVICE. The word comes from the Latin word for "new." It means a new monk or a new nun. Novices undergo training and "spiritual formation" in preparation for making vows. If a novice has been accepted into a religious order and given a religious habit, then he or she is a monk or a nun in the broad sense of the term.

NUN. A member of a religious community of women. The strictest use of the term means women who live a cloistered, contemplative life and have taken solemn perpetual vows (vows until death). The broad sense of the term includes new nuns (novices) and nuns who have made temporary vows.

NUNNERY. A convent. A community of nuns.

OBELISK. A four-sided, monolithic pillar which tapers as it rises and terminates in a pyramid. It is associated with pagan religions. There is a Roman obelisk in the square in front of Saint Peter's Basilica.

OFFICE. Position of trust and authority with specified duties.

OFFICE OF THE INQUISITION (Holy Office). This is located in the Vatican. In 1965 its name was changed to "The Congregation for the Doctrine of the Faith." It is presently headed by Cardinal Ratzinger.

OIL OF CATECHUMENS. Holy oil which is used in baptism. (See "Holy Oils")

OIL OF THE SICK. Holy oil which is used in the sacramental anointing of the sick. (See "Holy Oils")

ORDERS. (See "Sacrament") The sacrament of holy orders. Ordination of a deacon, priest or bishop.

ORDINARY. A cleric with ordinary jurisdiction over a specified territory. Bishops, abbots, and the Pope are also called ordinaries.

ORDINATION. (See "Sacrament") The sacrament of holy orders. To invest with ministerial functions. Deacons, priests and bishops are ordained.

ORIGINAL SIN. The sin which the human race inherited from Adam.

OUR FATHER (Pater Noster). The Lord's Prayer.

PALM SUNDAY. Blessed palms are a sacramental for liturgical use. (See "Sacramentals") Palms which have been blessed are distributed to the people to commemorate Jesus' triumphal entry into Jerusalem when the crowds waved palm branches to honor Him. It is traditional for people to take the palms home and keep them. They are often made into crosses. (The fresh palms are pliable and can be bent into different shapes.) Some palms are reserved by the priests so that they can be burned to provide ashes for Ash Wednesday of the following year.

PAPAL BULL. A papal letter which carries a special seal (a *bulla*) because of the importance of its subject matter.

PASCHAL CANDLE. A large Easter candle which contains five grains of incense, representing the five wounds of Christ. It is blessed on Holy Saturday (the day before Easter). It is used in the liturgical blessing of baptismal water. During the Paschal season it is kept in the sanctuary and lighted during liturgical services.

PASCHAL SEASON. The 56 days from Holy Saturday to the Saturday following Pentecost.

PATEN. It has the appearance of a saucer and is used to cover the chalice. It must be gold-plated or solid gold. The paten is consecrated by a bishop or his delegate, using chrism. The Communnion wafers which will be consecrated during Mass are placed on the paten.

PATRON SAINT. A saint who is invoked as a special intercessor for an individual or group of people. There are patron saints for countries, states of life, specific circumstances, etc. For example, St. Joseph is the patron saint of carpenters; St. Blaise is the patron saint of people with throat ailments; St. Benedict is the patron saint of monks and homeless people; and St. Jude is the saint to invoke for "lost causes" such as a family member who seems to be an incurable alcoholic.

PENANCE. (1) The Sacrament of Penance, which is also called Confession or the Sacrament of Reconciliation. (2) Punishment or voluntary suffering by means of which a person atones for sins. A person may do penance to atone for their own sins or for the sins of someone else (including deceased loved ones who may be in Purgatory). (See "Atone" and "Confession")

PENITENT. (1) In the Sacrament of Penance (Confession), a penitent is a person who confesses his or her sins and seeks absolution from the priest. (2) In the more general usage, the term means a person who repents for their sins and does something to expiate their guilt. According to Catholic doctrine, when God forgives sins He may still require that the sinner atone for those sins by suffering (either here on earth or else in Purgatory). Penitents may endure voluntary suffering now in order to avoid having to suffer in Purgatory later. Sometimes the penances of penitents may seem to be extreme. On Good Friday, penitents in some countries have processions through the streets, whipping themselves as they walk. (See "Expiate" and "Good Friday")

PENTECOST. The seventh Sunday after Easter.

PERPETUAL ADORATION OF THE BLESSED SACRAMENT. This is continual adoration of a large, consecrated Host which is displayed in a monstrance. People take turns so that somebody is always in the chapel or church, worshiping the Host. (See "Monstrance")

PERPETUAL VOW. A vow which is made until death.

PILGRIMAGE. A journey to a sacred place as an act of devotion or penance. In the Middle Ages, confessors sometimes required penitents to make pilgrimages. Pilgrimages are often made to the Holy Land, the Vatican, famous shrines, and sites where there have been apparitions. (See "Apparitions" and "Holy Land")

POCKET ROSARY. A rosary with only one decade (in a circle), a medal of Mary and a crucifix. People keep it in their pocket. If they want to pray the rosary without being noticed, they just put their hand in their pocket. One variation of the pocket rosary is the finger rosary. It is small, with the beads touching each other. It is often made of metal and looks like a ring.

POSTULANT. A man or woman who is taking the first steps towards becoming a monk or a nun. Postulants receive training in religious life. The period of postulancy enables the superiors of the religious community to determine whether or not the postulant is a suitable candidate for becoming a novice. (See "Novice")

PRIEST. According to the Catholic Church, a Catholic priest is a mediator between the people and God, and he offers a true sacrifice (the Sacrifice of the Mass) to God. Priests are ordained by bishops.

PROPITIATION. To atone for wrongdoing. To appease the person who has been offended by the wrongdoing. (See "Atonement")

PROPITIATORY. Something which propitiates. The Mass is said to be a propitiatory sacrifice which appeases God the Father and atones for the sins of the people.

PURGATORY. According to the Catholic Church, when God forgives sins He may still require that the sinner pay for his or her sins by suffering either here on earth or else in Purgatory. In Purgatory, the souls of the just are purified so that they can enter Heaven. They atone for their sins by willingly accepting God's just penalty of suffering. The degree of suffering is proportional to the degree of sinfulness. The suffering of the souls in Purgatory can be shortened by means of good works done on their behalf. These include having Masses said for them and earning indulgences on their behalf. It is traditional to give money to priests who say Masses on behalf of deceased loved ones. In modern times, earning indulgences is done primarily through special prayers and religious practices which are indulgenced. (The Catholic Church grants specific indulgences to people who do these things.) During the Middle Ages, indulgences were sold for money. This was a catalyst which helped cause the Reformation. Martin Luther began as a Catholic priest who strongly objected to the practice of selling indulgences.

RECONCILIATION (Confession). (See "Sacrament") According to Catholic doctrine, people who commit mortal sins after they are baptized are required to confess their sins to a qualified priest in order to receive absolution from their sins. This is also known as the Sacrament of Penance.

RELICS. A first-class relic is part of a saint's body. A second-class relic is something worn by or used by the saint during his or her life. A third-class relic is any other kind of object (for example, a piece of cloth which has touched a piece of a saint's bone). When an altar is consecrated, a relic of a martyr is placed in the altar stone. (See

"Altar Stone")

RELIGIOUS. A monk or a nun.

RELIQUARY. A special container for holding relics.

REMISSION OF SIN. The forgiveness of sin. According to the Catholic Church, if a mortal sin has been remitted, God pardons the sinner and removes the sentence of eternal punishment (hell). However, the sinner may still have to endure temporal punishment in order to pay for the sin. This requires suffering either here on earth or else in Purgatory. (See "Purgatory" and "Temporal Punishment")

REPARATION FOR SIN. When Jesus Christ voluntarily died on the cross, He satisfied the legitimate demands of God the Father. He made amends for the sinful wrongdoing of mankind. He repaired the breach caused by these offenses. This is called the Atonement.

ROMAN CURIA. Administrative and judicial offices which are located in the Vatican. They assist the Pope in directing the operations of the Catholic Church.

ROME. The Vatican is located in the city of Rome. It is known as the See of Peter, the Apostolic See, and the Holy See. Because the city of Rome is the location of the Pope and the men who direct the operations of the Catholic Church, the term "Rome" is used to refer to the Vatican. It is also used to refer to the Roman Catholic Church.

ROSARY. Traditional prayers in honor of the Virgin Mary which are said using a string of beads. There are five sets of decades. Each decade consists of one large bead and ten small beads. The "Our Father" (Lord's Prayer) is said on the large beads. The "Hail Mary" is said on the small beads. (The words of the "Hail Mary" are: "Hail Mary full of grace, the Lord is with thee. Blessed art thou among women and blessed is the fruit of thy womb, Jesus. Holy Mary, mother of God, pray for us sinners, now and at the hour of our death.") The five decades are joined to form a circle. A short string of beads is attached to the circle of beads. Traditional prayers are said on these beads before praying the five decades. There is a crucifix at the end of the short string of beads. There is a medal of Mary which connects the short string of beads with the circle of five decades of beads. The full rosary prayer consists of fifteen decades. In order to pray fifteen decades, people pray through the rosary beads three times. Each series of five decades is associated with five "mysteries" and it is traditional to meditate upon these mysteries while praying the rosary (or to at least mention the title associated with a mystery before praying a decade of beads). There are five joyful mysteries (such as the Annunciation, when the angel Gabriel announced to Mary that she would be the mother of the Lord Jesus). There are five sorrowful mysteries (such as the Crucifixion). There are five glorious mysteries (such as the Assumption of Mary into Heaven). The Catholic Church gives indulgences to people who pray the rosary. Some people wear rosaries like a necklace (usually under their clothes) or hang them from the mirror in their car. It is said that the rosary is powerful for protection from demons.

ROSARY BRACELET. One decade of the rosary, joined to form a circle which can be worn as a bracelet.

ROSARY NOVENA. Praying the full rosary (all fifteen decades), with some additional prayers, on nine consecutive occasions. It can also be done by praying five decades of the rosary on 27 consecutive occasions. (Five decades is a third of the full 15 decades. Nine times three is 27.)

ROSARY PROMISES. Our Lady of Fatima gave 15 promises to people who recite the rosary. These include promises that the entire celestial court will intercede for them during their life and at the hour of their death; they will not die without receiving the sacraments; at the moment of death they will share in the merits of the saints; and if they go to Purgatory, Mary will deliver them from it. In addition, the Catholic Church grants indulgences to Catholics who recite the rosary.

SABBATINE PRIVILEGE. An apparition of the Virgin Mary promised that if people wear the brown scapular, then if they go to Purgatory when they die, she will get them out on the Saturday after their death. According to tradition, in order to receive this benefit it is also necessary to pray the rosary and avoid sexual immorality.

SACRAMENT. According to the Catholic Church, Jesus Christ instituted the sacraments in order to give invisible grace and inward sanctification to the souls of people who faithfully participate in them. The Catholic Church recognizes seven sacraments. They are baptism, confirmation, Eucharist (Holy Communion), penance (confession, or sacrament of reconciliation), orders (ordination), matrimony (marriage), and anointing of the sick (extreme unction, or the last rites). Sacraments are rituals which use physical objects (such as bread, water, and incense) in order to receive spiritual benefits. The effectiveness of the sacraments is due to the rituals that are performed.

SACRAMENT OF RECONCILIATION (Sacrament of Penance). (See "Sacrament") According to Catholic doctrine, people who commit mortal sins after they are baptized are required to confess their sins to a qualified priest in order to receive absolution from their sins.

SACRAMENTALS. These are objects or actions which have the official approval of the Catholic Church. They include things such as holy water, medals, and scapulars. They also include pius practices such as praying rosaries, novenas, and litanies. Sacramentals are similar to sacraments because they use physical things in order to confer spiritual benefits. However, they were not instituted by Christ, and their effectiveness depends on the influence of the prayers of the participants. According to Catholic teaching, sacramentals benefit from the merits and prayers of the "Mystical Body of Christ." (See "Communion of Saints" and "Mystical Body of Christ")

SACRED HEART OF JESUS. Devotion to the Sacred Heart of Jesus was developed over the centuries by several mystics, the most recent being St. Margaret Mary Alacoque (1647-1690). There is a picture representing the Sacred Heart of Jesus. It shows Jesus with His chest open, His heart exposed, flames above His heart, and light coming out of His heart.

SACRED HEART PROMISES. Saint Margaret Mary Alacoque had an apparition of Jesus. He gave her 12 promises for people who are devoted to His Sacred Heart. One of them is the promise for people who observe the "Devotion of First Fridays." According to that promise, if Catholics receive Communion on the First Friday of nine consecutive months, then they will have the grace of final repentance; they will not die without receiving the sacraments; they will not be displeasing to Jesus when they die; and the Sacred Heart of Jesus will be their refuge.

SACRED HOST. A large, round wafer used by the priest when saying Mass. It is consecrated during the Mass.

SACRISTY. A room where the priest puts on his vestments. It is usually attached to the church and located near the altar. (See "Vestments")

SAINT. In the New Testament, the term "saint" applies to all Christians. The Catholic Church has restricted the use of the word to men and women of heroic virtue who have been traditionally recognized as saints or who have been canonized. According to the Catholic Church, saints may be publicly invoked. Prayers and petitions may be addressed to them. They may be publicly venerated.

SAINT ANNE'S OIL. According to tradition, Saint Anne is the mother of the Virgin Mary. In Canada there is a famous shrine in her honor, called Saint Anne de Beaupre. On the feast day of Saint Anne they have the blessing of the sick. There are reports of people being healed as a result. Oil from the shrine is said to be effective for healing sick people. Bottles of Saint Anne's oil can be purchased.

SAINT BENEDICT MEDAL.   Saint Benedict is the patron saint of monks, homeless people and people who have been poisoned. Indulgences have been given to Catholics who wear this medal. It has a picture of Saint Benedict, a cross, and a prayer of exorcism. It is said to protect people from evil. The "Blessing of Saint Maurus over the Sick" is done using the Saint Benedict Medal. There is a ritual which includes standard prayers and responses. Reportedly many sick people have been healed as a result of this blessing. Some people put a Saint Benedict Medal over the doorway of their home for protection.

SAINT BLAISE BLESSING.   On the feast day of St. Blaise, there is a special blessing of throats. Two candles are consecrated by a prayer. A priest holds the candles in a crossed position and touches the throats of the people with them. As he touches their throats, he says a standard prayer asking God to deliver the people from illnesses of the throat, through the intercession of St. Blaise. In some places, instead of using two candles, the priest touches the wick of a small candle with consecrated oil. He then uses the wick of the candle to touch the throats of the people.

SAINT CHRISTOPHER MEDAL.   Saint Christopher is the patron saint for travel, automobiles, and bachelors. His medal is very popular. It shows St. Christopher carrying the child Jesus on his shoulder. According to tradition, St. Christopher was a large young man who carried people across a dangerous river. One day he carried a child across the river. It turned out to be Jesus Christ in the form of a child.

SAINT ELMO'S BELT.   A belt made of metal with pieces that stick out. It can go around the waist, the thigh or the leg. The metal digs into a person's body and causes pain. This has been used as a form of penance, to mortify the body and to atone for sin.

SAINT PETER'S BASILICA.   A basilica (special kind of church) which adjoins the Pope's palace.

SCAPULAR.   (1) As part of the habit of a monk or nun, it is two strips of cloth joined across the shoulders.   (2) The Catholic Church has officially approved 18 different kinds of small scapulars which can be worn under the clothing. They can be worn by lay people as well as by religious (monks and nuns). These are two small pieces of cloth which are joined by strings. They are worn around the neck, under the clothing. Two of the most popular scapulars are the brown scapular and the green scapular. (See "Brown Scapular" and "Green Scapular")

SEVEN SACRAMENTS.   (See "Sacrament") The seven sacraments were defined by the Council of Trent on March 3, 1547. They are baptism, confirmation, Eucharist (Holy Communion), penance (confession, or sacrament of reconciliation), orders (ordination), matrimony (marriage), and anointing of the sick (extreme unction, or the last rites).

SHRINE. Shrines are located at sacred places. They may be where a saint is buried, or where there was an apparition of Mary. Pilgrims come to shrines. Shrines can be as small as a box which contains relics or statues or other holy images. They can be as large as the Basilica of the National Shrine of the Immaculate Conception, which is a huge building containing a large church and many chapels.

SIGN OF THE CROSS. Tracing the pattern of a cross on a person's body. The right hand goes first to the forehead, then to the breast, then to the left and right shoulders. When it goes to the forehead, the person says "In the name of the Father." When it goes to the breast, the person says, "and of the Son". When it goes to the left and right shoulders the person says "and of the Holy Spirit." It is traditional to make the sign of the cross, using holy water, when entering a Catholic Church.

SISTINE CHAPEL. This is the main chapel of the Vatican Palace. It is as large as a church. It features statues and paintings by famous artists, including Botticelli. Michelangelo painted the ceiling. This is the Pope's private chapel and the place where the conclaves for papal elections are held. The altar is inlaid with mother of pearl. Only the Pope is allowed to use it.

STATE OF GRACE. If a person is free from mortal sin then he or she is said to be in a state of grace. This makes them pleasing to God. In order for people to go to Heaven, they must be in a state of grace when they die.

STIGMATA. A phenomenon in which the wounds of Christ appear on a person. They are painful and bleeding. The stigmata are usually the wounds in the hands, feet and side. Sometimes they include the wounds in the back from whipping, and the wounds in the forehead from the crown of thorns. Saint Francis of Assisi and Blessed Padre Pio had the stigmata. Some of the people who see apparitions of Mary also have the stigmata. Over 300 cases of stigmatization are known, including more than 60 canonized saints.

STIGMATIC. A person who has the stigmata.

TABERNACLE. An ornate box in which the consecrated Communion wafers are kept. It is lined with precious metal or silk. The Tabernacle is kept in a prominent place so that Catholics can pray in front of it. This encourages devotion to the Blessed Sacrament.

TEMPORAL PUNISHMENT. According to the Catholic Church, when God forgives sins He may still require that the sinner atone for his or her sins by suffering either here on earth or else in Purgatory. (See "Purgatory")

TIARA. The Pope's crown.

TRADITION. According to Catholic doctrine, tradition is divine revelation which is not contained in the Bible, and which has been passed down through the Catholic Church. Tradition is considered to be as authoritative as Scripture.

VATICAN. The Pope's palace, Saint Peter's Basilica, and surrounding buildings which are used for administering the affairs of the Catholic Church. It is located in Rome. The Pope has the largest palace in the world. The term "Vatican" is also used to mean the power structure of the Catholic Church.

VATICAN CITY. Territory in Rome which is under the immediate jurisdiction of the Pope. Its government is based on Canon Law. It is a state which enjoys all of the privileges of a sovereign power. It has diplomatic relations with other nations and makes treaties (concordats) with them. Cardinals are citizens of Vatican City in addition to being citizens of their own countries.

VENERATION. Special honor given to Mary and the saints. Veneration can take many forms. It includes publicly praying to Mary and the saints and invoking their assistance. (This can be accompanied by kneeling in front of statues of them, or placing lit votive candles in front of their statues.) It includes carrying statues of them in solemn processions, and the liturgical crowning of statues of Mary. It includes having pictures of them or wearing medals or scapulars associated with them. It includes praying novenas, litanies, rosaries, and chaplets in their honor. It includes studying their lives and writings and imitating their virtues. It includes naming children after them. (See "Novena," "Litany," "Rosary," and "Chaplet")

VENERATION OF IMAGES. Reverence given to images of Jesus, Mary, and the saints. These can be statues, paintings, mosaics, etc. Catholic Churches are required to have such images. Catholics are encouraged to have them in their homes and to honor them. Catholics can also venerate images by wearing medals or scapulars which have images on them.

VENIAL SIN. An offense against God which is not serious enough to destroy the supernatural life of the soul.

VESTMENTS. Special garments worn by the clergy when administering the sacraments or otherwise exercising official priestly duties.

VICAR. A clergyman who acts as a substitute for another clergyman, exercising his office and acting in his name and with his authority.

VICAR OF CHRIST. A title for the Pope indicating that the Pope acts for Christ and in the place of Christ.

VICTIM SOUL. A person who willingly endures suffering in order to atone for the sins of other people. Some apparitions of Mary have asked people to be victim souls. When people agree to do it, they are then afflicted with great suffering. This can be through disease, the stigmata, or other things.

VISION. Something which is seen supernaturally. It may be seen with open eyes, or seen in the mind. An apparition is different from a vision. An apparition is something which is actually present, and which can be seen through supernatural means. A vision may be a picture rather than a presence.

VOTIVE CANDLES. Candles which are burned before a statue or a shrine in order to honor Jesus, Mary, or a saint. It is customary for shrines to have candles. People who light them pay money for the privilege of using the candles. Candles are one form of votive offering. (See "Votive Offering")

VOTIVE OFFERING. An object offered in honor of Jesus, Mary or a saint. It can be a form of petition for a favor asked for, or an act of appreciation for a favor which has been granted. The object may be anything which is of value to the donor. In some places it is traditional for people to pay to put an advertisement in a Catholic newspaper publicly thanking a saint for "favors granted." This is often done for Saint Jude, the patron saint of "lost causes."

WORDS OF ABSOLUTION. The words ritually used by a priest to absolve the sins of a penitent during the sacrament of penance (confession).

WORDS OF CONSECRATION. A verbal formula which is used by the priest during Mass. According to Catholic doctrine, when the priest says these words, the bread and wine literally become the body, blood, soul, and divinity of Jesus Christ. This is called the consecration of the bread and wine. The consecrated bread and wine are referred to as the Eucharist or the Blessed Sacrament. The Catholic Church uses Communion wafers instead of regular bread.

ZUCCHETTO. A small round skullcap worn by Catholic clergymen. The Pope wears white. Cardinals wear scarlet. Bishops wear purple. Priests wear black.

APPENDIX 1
RELEVANT ARTICLES
AND PICTURES

1. The Two Most Corrupt Popes
Pope John XII
http://orthodox.truepath.com/articles/catholicism/romanbishop/
JohnXII.htm

Pope Alexander VI
http://orthodox.truepath.com/articles/catholicism/romanbishop/
AlexanderVI.htm

The Borgia Pope (Alexander VI)
http://www.crimelibrary.com/borgia/borgiapopes.htm

2. Some Other Corrupt Popes
Pope Benedict VIII
http://orthodox.truepath.com/articles/catholicism/romanbishop/
BenedictVIII.htm

Pope Benedict IX
http://orthodox.truepath.com/articles/catholicism/romanbishop/
BenedictIX.htm

Pope Clement VI
http://orthodox.truepath.com/articles/catholicism/romanbishop/
ClementVI.htm

Pope Julius II
http://orthodox.truepath.com/articles/catholicism/romanbishop/
JuliusII.htm

3. Development of Papal Power and Authority
The Development of Papal Power
http://www.geocities.com/Athens/Parthenon/2104/papal_power.html

Pope Gregory VII
http://orthodox.truepath.com/articles/catholicism/romanbishop/
GregoryVII.htm

Pope Innocent III
http://orthodox.truepath.com/articles/catholicism/romanbishop/
InnocentIII.htm

4. Forged Church Documents
The Historical Use and Influence of Forgeries
http://orthodox.truepath.com/articles/catholicism/forgeries/
HistoricalInfluence.htm

Forged "Proof" (links to 28 articles about forged documents)
http://orthodox.truepath.com/menu/catholic/FalseDocuments.htm

5. The Albigensian Massacre (Crusade)
The Massacre of the Albigensians
http://orthodox.truepath.com/articles/catholicism/oppression/
AlbigensianMassacre.htm

6. The Inquisition
Fourth Lateran Council: Canon 3 on Heresy
http://orthodox.truepath.com/articles/catholicism/oppression/
LateranCouncilHeresy.htm

The Roman Inquisition
http://orthodox.truepath.com/articles/catholicism/oppression/
RomanInquisition.htm

The Spanish Inquisition
http://orthodox.truepath.com/articles/catholicism/oppression/
SpanishInquisition.htm

The Inquisition in the New World
http://orthodox.truepath.com/articles/catholicism/oppression/
newworldinquisition.htm

7. The Crusades
The Christian Crusades
http://gbgm umc.org/umw/bible/crusades.stm

The Fall of Jerusalem
http://crusades.boisestate.edu/1st/28.htm

The Fourth Crusade (the pillaging of Constantinople)
http://orthodox.truepath.com/articles/catholicism/oppression/
FourthCrusade.htm

The Crusades
http://www.reconciliationwalk.org/crusades.htm

Catholic Oppression (numerous articles about the Inquisition, Crusades, Massacres etc.)
http://orthodox.truepath.com/menu/catholic/ReligiousOppression.htm

The Reconciliation Walk
http://www.soon.org.uk/page15.htm

A Crusade of Contrition (article from *The Jerusalem Post*)
http://www.reconciliationwalk.org/jpost970626.htm

8. Opposing the Bible
Rules issued by the Council of Trent regarding forbidden books. The general public was forbidden to read the Bible. Only certain special people were allowed to read it.
http://www.fordham.edu/halsall/mod/trent booksrules.html

The Bible was banned by the Inquisition. It was on their Index of Forbidden Books.
http://palimpsest.stanford.edu/byform/mailing lists/bookarts/1998/01/
msg00284.html

William Tyndale translated the Bible into English. His Bibles were burned. Tyndale was burned at the stake. Between 1400 and 1557 over 1,000 English men and women were burned at the stake for the sake of the Gospel.
http://www.williamtyndale.com/0crimesofwilliamtyndale.htm

More information about Tyndale and the Bible. When the King of England authorized an English translation of the Bible, it was kept in a church. From dawn to dusk that church was crowded with people. As long as there was light, men took turns reading the Bible out loud while the crowds listened.
http://justus.anglican.org/resources/bio/260.html

Information about Tyndale and Wycliffe
http://www.prca.org/books/portraits/tyndale.htm

The Catholic Church's historical and theological approach to the Bible
http://www.angelfire.com/ky/dodone/Bible.html

The burning of John Hus and his books. (Hus believed the Bible. He influenced Tyndale.)
http://www.lawbuzz.com/cherished_rights/freedom_speech/hus_burns.htm

9. Quotes from Popes who Exalted the Papacy
Popes said that the popes are exalted above all of mankind
http://orthodox.truepath.com/articles/catholicism/deification/PapalQuotes.htm

Popes said that there is no salvation apart from the pope
http://www.reachingcatholics.org/pastpopes.html

10. Worship of the Eucharist
Eucharistic Adoration: Worship or Idolatry?
http://www.reachingcatholics.org/eucharistic_adoration.html

11. Mary
Past Popes Taught Destructive Heresies (no salvation without Mary)
http://www.reachingcatholics.org/pastpopes.html

Do You Know Mary?
http://www.reachingcatholics.org/knowmary.html

Mary Who?
http://www.reachingcatholics.org/marywho.html

Hail Mary?
http://www.reachingcatholics.org/hailmarymd.html

Mary and Catholicism
http://members.aol.com/jasonte/mary.htm

Mary in Roman Catholicism
http://members.aol.com/jasonte2/mary2.htm

12. Statues which Dominate Chapels
Chapel of Our Lady of Siluva (picture and prayers)
http://www.nationalshrine.com/NAT_SHRINE/tour_u32.htm

Chapel of Our Lady of the Miraculous Medal (picture and prayers)
http://www.nationalshrine.com/NAT_SHRINE/tour_u04.htm

Large statue of Mary with many votive candles burning in front of it
(picture and prayers)
http://www.nationalshrine.com/NAT_SHRINE/tour_c37.htm

Picture of Chapel Honoring Apparition of Mary to St. Catherine Laboure
http://www.cammonline.org/pagesShrineTour/shrine05En.html

13. Infant of Prague
Article with pictures of the statue (clothed and unclothed)
http://religion cults.com/childjesus/prague.htm

Article with picture of cardinal carrying the statue
http://www.medjugorjecenter.org/prague/page2.htm

Article with several pictures and history of the statue
http://karmel.at/prag jesu/english/eng/jezuleen.htm

Article with pictures showing nuns changing the clothes of the statue
http://karmel.at/prag jesu/english/eng/saticken.htm

Article with pictures showing details of the crown and some of the clothes
http://karmel.at/prag jesu/english/eng/muzejen.htm

History of the Infant Jesus of Prague
http://www.cwo.com/ ~ pentrack/catholic/infhist.html

14. Statues with Gold Crowns (Some Wearing Expensive Clothing)
This article has four pictures of statues wearing gold crowns. Three of
them are wearing expensive and elaborate clothing. It also has pictures
of two processions with statues. One of them is the candlelight procession
in Fatima, Portugal with multitudes of people.
http://www.aloha.net/ ~ mikesch/baruch.htm

Pictures of ceremony for crowning a statue by 5th grade class of a Catholic
school
http://www.stfrancisvernon.org/Crowning5th.htm

15. Processions with Statues
Millions in Mexico Gather for Marian Feast (2½ million people, October
1999)
http://www.cwnews.com/news/viewrec.cfm?RefNum = 11317

Our Lady of Guadalupe (8 million people in Mexico City,   December
2001)
http://www.e3mil.com/vm/index.asp?vm_id = 1&art_id = 930

Pictures of American Hispanics having local processions for Our Lady
of Guadalupe
http://hemi.ps.tsoa.nyu.edu/archive/studentwork/colony/reed/
procession.htm
http://www.laprensa sandiego.org/archieve/december14/PARADE.HTM

16. The Brown Scapular
The Brown Scapular of Our Lady of Mount Carmel
http://www.rc.net/lansing/ctk/cc/ocds1.html

The Brown Scapular
http://www.cin.org/saints/brownsca.html

The Rosary, Brown Scapular and the Sabbatine Privilege
http://olrl.org/pray/rosary.html

17. Rosary Promises
Fifteen Promises of the Virgin Mary to those who recite the Rosary
Indulgences promised by the Catholic Church for praying the rosary
http://rosarycreations.com/rosarypromises.htm

15 Promises of the Rosary and 12 Promises of the Sacred Heart
http://www.memorare.com/devotions/promises.html

18. The Miraculous Medal
The Miraculous Medal (picture and description of apparition)
http://www.cammonline.org/pages/miraculousMedal.html

Apparition Chapel in Paris (2 million pilgrims per year)
http://www.cammonline.org/pages/appritionChapel.html

Novena Prayers to Our Lady of the Miraculous Medal
http://www.cammonline.org/pages/novena.html

19. Thomas Aquinas
Thomas Aquinas relied on forged documents but he thought they were
genuine
http://www.christiantruth.com/forgeries.html

Thomas Aquinas (the *Catholic Encyclopedia*)
http://www.newadvent.org/cathen/14663b.htm

Ecstasy (the *Catholic Encyclopedia*)
http://www.newadvent.org/cathen/05277a.htm

20. Purgatory
Purgatory: An Essential Roman Catholic Doctrine
http://www.reachingcatholics.org/purgatory.html

21. Sale of Indulgences
Official Instructions for the Sale of Indulgences
http://www.aloha.net/ ~ mikesch/instruc.htm

Tetzel's Sale of Indulgences
http://www.aloha.net/ ~ mikesch/tetzel.htm

22. Priests Have Raped Nuns
NOTE: This is happening today. It demonstrates the credibility of statements by Protestant historians that similar events occurred throughout much of the history of the Catholic Church. A former Catholic priest has also written about this problem. Peter de Rosa is a practicing Catholic who did research in the Vatican Archives while he was a priest. His book *Vicars of Christ* gives extensive quotations from official church documents which describe the sexual immorality of Catholic clergy. One of the documents tells how a group of priests went into a convent and raped the nuns. It was brutal. The quotation comes from an official report which was written for the Pope.

Nuns who were raped by priests are filing official complaints (August 2002)
http://www2.bostonherald.com/news/local_regional/nun08202002.htm

Some priests have been raping nuns (National Catholic Reporter, March 2001)
http://www.natcath.com/NCR_Online/archives/031601/031601a.htm

Some priests and bishops have been sexually exploiting nuns.
http://www.guardian.co.uk/Distribution/Redirect_Artifact/0,4678,0
460287,00.html

The Vatican was given a report about priests who were sexually abusing nuns. Nothing was done about it for seven years. Finally in 2001 the report was leaked to the press. One of the cases involved a priest who got a nun pregnant and then forced her to have an abortion. She died as a result of the abortion.
http://news.bbc.co.uk/1/hi/world/europe/1234268.stm

The Vatican acknowledged that some priests have raped nuns. (This happened after the report was leaked to the press, so it had already become public knowledge.)
http://www.cnn.com/2001/WORLD/europe/11/22/pope.apology/

Statement by the National Coalition of American Nuns. This focuses on the problem in Africa (where it is especially severe) but it also says that priests have raped nuns in 23 countries including the United States, Italy, Brazil, India, Ireland and the Philippines.
http://www.calltoaccountability.org/coalition.htm

Demonstrations demanding that the Vatican stop priests from raping nuns
http://www.calltoaccountability.org/071401Advisory.htm
http://www.calltoaccountability.org/071001Advisory.htm

A history of how celibacy became mandatory for priests. It includes information about married priests who were imprisoned and their wives and children were sold into slavery.
http:/www.rentapriest.com/history.htm

A ministry to help children whose fathers are priests
http://www.marriedpriests.org/HOLYINNOCENTS.htm

Legal guidelines for women whose children were fathered by priests
http://www.marriedpriests.org/Alegalguide.htm

23. Bishops Allowed Sexually Abusive Priests to Remain in Office
NOTE: Bishops today not only allowed child-molesting priests to remain in office, they protected the priests and covered up their crimes. This demonstrates the credibility of statements by Protestant historians that sexual abuse by priests occurred throughout much of the history of the Catholic Church.

Bishops covered up sexual crimes of priests
http://www.washingtonpost.com/wp dyn/articles/A9255 2002Jun6.html

A summary of some key priest rape cases involving boys and girls
http://www.angelfire.com/de/knowledgeoftruth/celibacy.html

A web page with links to many articles about priest sex abuse cases and links to some web sites with extensive coverage of such cases
http://www.vawnet.org/VNL/library/res_room/Clergy
SA2.html?where=library

Some articles about priests who sexually molested children and adolescents in the confessional (a place where Catholics go to confess their sins to a priest)
http://news.bbc.co.uk/1/hi/uk/52884.stm
http://www.boston.com/globe/spotlight/abuse/stories/
030602_xaverian.htm
http://www.freep.com/news/religion/priest22_20020622.htm
http://www.sexcriminals.com/news/11868/

24. Rules about Forbidden Foods
NOTE: Peter de Rosa's book *Vicars of Christ* has several references to Catholics being tortured by Inquisitors and killed as heretics because they ate meat during Lent. One man was killed for eating an egg during Lent.

According to Canon Law, Catholics are still required to abstain from eating meat every Friday.
http://www.catholic pages.com/life/fridaymeat.asp

American Bishops met to discuss whether or not to require Catholics to abstain from eating meat on all Fridays (1997)
http://www.trosch.org/for/the/abs main.htm

Rules about eating meat on "meatless days" if Catholics have dinner with non-Catholics
http://www.cmri.org/adsum02 1a.html

Eating fish on Fridays
http://www.cin.org/users/james/questions/q034.htm

Days when fasting is required and what Catholics are allowed to eat on those days
http://www.traditio.com/cal.htm

25. Saint Peter's, Necropolis, Circus Maximus
Travel narrative describes Saint Peter's (with pictures), Necropolis and
Circus Maximus
http://www.aerenlund.dk/rom/rome_day3.html

Description of Saint Peter's (with pictures) mentions tours of Necropolis
http://free.rmnet.it/ ~ pellegrino/ctv/basilica.htm

Gladiators, the Roman Circus and Christians
http://www.christianity.com/partner/Article_Display_Page/
0,,PTID4859%7CCHID45%7CCIID142387,00.html

Tacitus on the Christians (describes the martyrdom of Christians in the
Circus Maximus)
http://www.livius.org/cg cm/christianity/tacitus.html

26. Overview of Church History
Two Millennia of Church History
http://www.foigm.org/IMG/millhist.htm
http://www.christianity.com/CC/article/
0,,PTID306608|CHID556136|CIID1397350,00.html

27. Overview of Recent Canon Law
Has Roman Catholicism Changed? An Overview of Recent Canon Law
http://www.reachingcatholics.org/rcchanged.html

28. Other Subjects
Jesus Christ Is Sufficient to Save Sinners Completely
http://www.reachingcatholics.org/save_sinners.html

Why Catholics Don't Understand Sin
http://www.reachingcatholics.org/understand.html

It Is Finished!
http://www.pro gospel.org/articles/finish.html

No One Can Merit the Unmerited Favor of God
http://www.reachingcatholics.org/unmerited.html

29. On-Line Book by Mary Ann Collins
The Spirit of Roman Catholicism: What Lies Behind the Modern Public Image?
http://www.catholicconcerns.com/Book01/Index.html

APPENDIX 2
HELPFUL WEB SITES

Just For Catholics
http://www.justforcatholics.org

Catholic Concerns
http://www.CatholicConcerns.com

Christians Evangelizing Catholics
This site has a "Glossary of Catholic Doctrine and Biblical
Rebuttal" where you can look up subjects alphabetically.
http://www.angelfire.com/ky/dodone/

Good News for Catholics
http://www.gnfc.org

Proclaiming the Gospel
http://www.pro-gospel.org

Berean Beacon
http://www.bereanbeacon.org

Reaching Catholics for Christ
http://www.reachingcatholics.org/mainpage.html

Mission To Catholics International
http://mtc.org/ ~ bart

Freedom from Catholicism
(At this site the article can be downloaded and there are links to
relevant articles.)
http://www.FreedomFromCatholicism.com